Cupcakes & Muffins

Ann Nicol

Publisher's Note: Raw or semi-cooked eggs should not be consumed by babies, toddlers, pregnant or breastfeeding women, the elderly or those suffering from a chronic illness.

Publisher & Creative Director: Nick Wells
Senior Project Editor: Catherine Taylor
Photography: Colin Bowling
Home economist and stylist: Ann Nicol
Copy Editor: Constance Novis
Art Director: Mike Spender
Layout Design: Dave Jones
Digital Design & Production: Chris Herbert
Proofreader: Dawn Laker

Special thanks to Digby Smith and Helen Wall, and to the following for supplying materials for photography:

For all cake-decorating supplies by mail order, such as paper cases, sugarpaste, fondant, icing colours and equipment and bakeware: Squires Group, Squires House, 3 Waverley Lane, Farnham, Surrey, GU9 8BB. Tel: 0845 22 55 67 1/2. www.squires-shop.com

For bakeware, muffin tins and trays and paper cases by mail order:
Lakeland, Alexandria Buildings, Windermere, Cumbria, LA23 1BQ. Tel: 01539 488 100. www.lakeland.co.uk

This is a **FLAME TREE** Book

FLAME TREE PUBLISHING
Crabtree Hall, Crabtree Lane
Fulham, London SW6 6TY
United Kingdom
www.flametreepublishing.com

Flame Tree is part of The Foundry Creative Media Company Limited

First published 2010

Cupcakes & Muffins

Quick and Easy, Proven Recipes

**FLAME TREE
PUBLISHING**

Contents

Teatime Treats...82

Sometimes, there is nothing better than dainty sandwiches and pretty cakes, washed down with lashings of tea. This section includes classic cakes in cupcake form – from the unrivalled Lemon Drizzle to Coffee & Walnut. Delightful aromatic and flavoursome creations include Crystallised Violet and Lemon & Cardamom cupcakes. You will be spoilt for choice for your afternoon tea!

Chocolate Delights................................124

The epitome of indulgence, chocolate deserves its own section. The perfect partner for fellow decadents such as fudge and toffee, it renders Chocolate Fudge Flake Muffins and Chocolate & Toffee Cupcakes to die for. Then there are the fruits and flavourings that give chocolate a different identity – why not try Mint Choc Chip or Chocolate & Orange Marbled Muffins? Of course, sometimes you just crave pure, unadulterated heaven, which you will find in Very Rich Chocolate Cupcakes.

For Parties & Special Occasions 168

Cupcakes are ideal for parties and celebrations, since they can be personalised and decorated in any way, and their individual form makes them easy for guests to pick up and consume, with no cutting necessary! From figurative designs ideal for kids' parties, such as Pirate Cupcakes, to beautiful and delicate designs for romantic and special occasions, such as Winter Wedding Cupcakes, you have a plethora of choices and a world of inspiration.

**Butterfly alternative: Pink Butterfly Cakes, page 122**

For Seasonal Celebrations 242

Whether you are having a Halloween party or are running out of ideas for Christmas gifts, the seasons and their celebrations offer many ideas for little cakes. Have a go at making the attractive decorations for Spring Daffodil Cupcakes, have fun with the glittery and metallic decorations for Sparkly Christmas Cupcakes, or simply savour the evocative flavours and aromas of Gingerbread Cupcakes or Honey Spice Cupcakes. Take some freshly baked cakes to visit family and relish the delighted faces.

Savoury Muffins 282

Do not forget that muffins lend themselves well to savoury ingredients. Nothing beats the aroma of freshly baked muffins – ideal for serving warm with butter for breakfast or a tasty snack. This section offers some fun and interesting ideas for savoury muffins, including Pizza Mini Muffins and moreish Peanut Butter Muffins. All kinds of vegetables can be used, such as courgettes, leeks and sweetcorn; and, of course, all are complemented well by the inclusion of cheese or bacon – mmm!

Sweet Muffins 308

Last but not least, we have sweet muffins – in addition to those featured in the chocolate section. Muffins, with their distinctive rustic tops, offer a heartier option than cupcakes; it is all about the cake rather than the decoration. The classics here include Blueberry Buttermilk and Choc Chip Cherry Muffins, but there are also all sorts of fantastic combinations, ranging from Rhubarb & Custard to Coconut & Lime.

Introduction

Why are cupcakes and muffins so popular? They seem to be on sale everywhere these days, but, as these little cakes are so quick and easy (you will find that most of the recipes in this book take under half an hour to bake), it is so simple to make your own. Cupcakes, fairy cakes and muffins are delightful and versatile – ideal for breakfast, an informal tea, a special occasion or for children's parties.

You will not only enjoy creating your own home-made masterpieces, but also, as shop-bought cakes are expensive, you will notice the difference in price. There is no comparison to the quality of home-made cakes and the fun to be had in making and baking them. You also have plenty of scope for decorating, so you can create tailor-made treats for all sorts of occasions.

As a gift or a centrepiece, a batch of cupcakes or muffins brings a personal touch to any celebration, from a wedding anniversary to a children's party. This book has cakes for every occasion, some very quick and easy, some requiring a little more patience. You will find cakes for birthdays, or simple sweet or savoury muffins that go well with a cup of tea. And some of these sweet ideas are ideal for packing away into lunchboxes.

Baking is a good way to introduce children to the art of cookery and these recipes will help to teach the basic techniques. Children also love the decorating part, and there are lots of ideas here to choose from.

If you are ever asked to bake for a charity stall or school fête, cupcakes and muffins are the quick and easy choice that will not break your budget. If you are short on time, I have included tips on preparing ahead and freezing to make life easy.

So what is the best part of baking cupcakes and muffins? Well, they give so much pleasure: you get a real sense of satisfaction when you create a fresh batch of delicious bakes, accompanied by the marvellous aroma of baking that fills your home; and just watch the delighted reaction when you give them to your friends and neighbours.

This book is aimed at both those new to baking and experienced bakers, and shows how to create these popular mini-cakes, from the right equipment and ingredients to the cake and its decoration. So choose a recipe that appeals, get out your mixing bowls and start baking!

How to Use This Book

If you are a first-time or less experienced baker, remember that there are no secrets to baking – just follow our simple step-by-step guides to ensure successful results. The choice is yours – you can make deep muffins, the shallower cupcakes and delicate fairy cakes, or mini muffins. The size of each cake will depend on the depth of your tins and how deeply you fill the paper cases.

Everybody loves home bakes and friends always welcome old favourites, but everyone loves to try new treats. This book is divided into sections that deal with different types of cakes, including family favourites and fairy cakes for teatime treats, luscious chocolate cakes, and small cakes decorated for special occasions such as birthdays, Mother's Day, weddings and Christmas. There is also a great selection of sweet and savoury muffins to choose from – the latter being delicious served warm for breakfast.

Baking and cake decoration involves many different techniques and a little skill is needed for certain cakes, but you will build up your confidence through practice. To help you achieve success every time, there are tips on choosing the right type of muffin and bun tins and paper liners. Using the very best ingredients is important, as are utensils and careful weighing and measuring. You will not achieve good results without first checking your oven for correct temperatures and exact timings (*see* opposite).

All methods and techniques are clearly explained with plenty of step-by-step photographs to help you achieve good results and you will find a set of patterns and templates at the back of this book to trace round onto clear greaseproof paper. These can be transferred to rolled-out icing by tracing round the pattern onto the icing with the tip of a sharp knife.

Check Your Oven

Each recipe begins with an oven setting, and it is important to preheat the oven to the correct temperature before placing the cakes in to bake. As well as preheating the oven, it is important to arrange the shelves in the correct position in the oven before you start. The best baking position for cupcakes is just above the centre of the oven and best results are achieved by baking only one tray at a time. If you bake two trays at once, you may find the lower tray will come out with flatter tops to the cakes.

Many of us have fan-assisted ovens. These circulate hot air round the oven and heat up very quickly. For fan ovens, you will need to reduce the temperature stated in the recipe by 10 per cent, which is usually 20°C. For example, if the stated temperature in a recipe is 180°C, reduce it to 160°C for a fan-assisted oven. However, ovens do vary, so do follow your manufacturer's instructions and get to know the way your oven heats. If your oven is too hot, the outsides of the cakes will burn before the interior has had time to cook. If it is too cool, the cakes may sink

or not rise evenly. Try not to open the oven door until at least halfway through the baking time, when the cakes have had time to rise and set, as a sudden drop in temperature will stop the cakes rising and they may sink.

Weighing and Measuring

All of the recipes in this book give metric and imperial measurements, but you must stick to one set only – i.e. only ever use either metric or imperial in one recipe, as they are not exact equivalents.

All spoon measurements should be used level (as opposed to 'heaped') for accuracy, and always use a recognised set of metric or imperial spoon measures for best results. Do not use domestic teaspoons and tablespoons as measures, as these may be deeper or shallower than a proper measuring spoon. Never estimate weights, as you will not achieve an accurate result.

Ingredients for baking should be weighed exactly and good kitchen scales are a vital piece of equipment for a baker. Old-fashioned scales with a pan and a set of weights or modern ones with a digital display screen are equally good, as long as they are accurate. A measuring jug is vital for liquids and it needs to be marked with small measures for smaller amounts.

What You Need

Trays and Cases

Metal Muffin Trays

Muffin trays come in different weights and sizes; they are generally available with six or 12 deep-set holes. When purchasing, buy the heaviest type you can – although these will be expensive, they produce the best results, as they have good heat distribution and do not buckle. Muffin trays can vary in the size and depth of hole, which obviously affects the eventual size of the muffin. If using trays without a nonstick finish, it is advisable to give these a light greasing before use. To grease trays, apply a thin film of melted vegetable margarine with a pastry brush or rub round the tin with kitchen paper and a little softened butter or margarine. You will normally need to line metal muffin trays with deep paper muffin cases or strips of baking parchment.

Silicone Muffin Trays and Cupcake Cases

These are flexible and produce very good results. Although they are sold as nonstick, it is still advisable to rub round

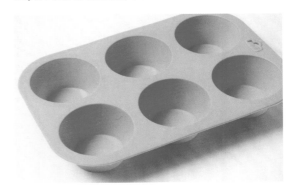

each hole or case with a little oil on kitchen paper to prevent sticking. Silicone cupcake cases come in many bright colours and, unlike paper cases, are reusable. Simply wash out any crumbs after use in soapy water and leave them to dry, or clean them in the dishwasher.

Fairy-cake trays

Also known as 'bun trays' or 'patty trays', these are similar to muffin trays but have shallower indentations for making smaller individual cakes. You will need to line each indentation with a paper fairy-cake case.

Mini-muffin trays

These have small individual holes that are half the size of holes in the big trays. They can be made of metal, but the silicone trays are particularly useful for mini muffins, as they turn out so easily and give a good shape.

Paper Cases

These come in many varieties, colours and shapes. It is advisable to buy the more expensive types, which are thicker and give a good shape to the cake as it rises. Oil and moisture is less likely to penetrate through the thicker cases, whereas it may show through the cheaper ones. Metallic gold, silver and coloured cupcake cases give good results and create a stunning effect for a special occasion. Cupcake cases also come in mini-muffin sizes. These may not be so easy to find but can be bought from mail-order cake decoration suppliers.

Baking Papers and Foil

Nonstick baking 'parchment' or 'paper' is useful for lining the bases of small tins or for drying out chocolate and sugarpaste shapes.

Greaseproof paper is needed for making triangular paper icing bags. Baking parchment can be used, but greaseproof paper is better, as it is thinner and more flexible.

Foil A large sheet of kitchen foil is handy for wrapping cakes or for protecting wrapped cakes in the freezer.

Equipment and Utensils for Baking

Electric Mixers

A handheld electric mixer makes quick work of whisking butter and sugar and is an invaluable aid for cake baking. A large tabletop mixer is useful if you are making larger quantities of muffins and is good for whisking frostings and buttercream in larger quantities. Do not be tempted to use a food processor for mixing small amounts, as it is easy to over-process and this may produce flat cakes.

Mixing Bowls

You will need a set of different size mixing bowls for beating

small and large amounts of mixture, making frostings and colouring icings.

Wooden Spoon

Keep an old-fashioned large wooden spoon aside for baking, for beating butters and creaming. Do not use one that has been used for frying savoury things like onions, as the flavours will taint the cake mixture.

Measuring Spoons

A set of standard measuring spoons for accurate measuring of small quantities of ingredients is vital. Sets of plastic or metal measures are sold just for this purpose. Remember that all spoon measures should be level and not to use cutlery such as kitchen tablespoons or teaspoons, as these sizes differ and may be inaccurate.

Cake Tester or Skewer

Use a small thin metal skewer for inserting into the centre of a cake to test if the cake is ready. This is a handy piece of equipment but, if you do not have one, a clean thin metal knitting needle may be used instead.

Pastry Brush

A pastry brush is used for brushing glazes over cakes and melted butter round tins. As brushes tend to wear out regularly and shed their bristles, keep a spare new brush to hand.

Palette Knives

A small and a large palette knife are ideal for many jobs, including loosening cakes from their tins, lifting cakes and swirling on buttercream icing. A palette knife with a cranked blade is useful for lifting small cakes or flat pieces of sugarpaste.

Kitchen Scissors

Scissors are essential for many small jobs, including cutting papers to size and snipping cherries, dried fruits or nuts into chunks.

Grater

A grater is useful for grating citrus zests, chocolate and marzipan. Choose one with a fine and a coarse side.

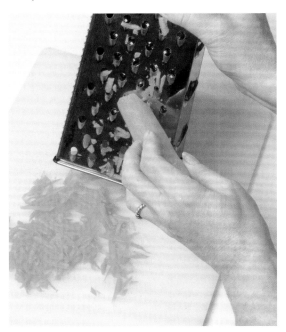

Sieves

Use a large wire sieve for sifting flour and dry ingredients together and keep a smaller one, ideally nylon, aside just for icing sugars.

Wire Racks

Racks are vital to allow air to circulate round the hot cakes to let them cool down quickly, which prevents them from becoming moist or soggy underneath.

Stamps and Cutters

Stamps and cutters for almost any imaginable shape can be bought from specialist cake and baking stores. They come in classic metal cookie-cutter styles, in plastic, or as plunger-style. If you do not have appropriate cutters, there are some templates at the back of this book that can be used instead. *See also* page 79.

Piping Bags and Nozzles

A nylon piping bag that comes with a set of five nozzles is a very useful piece of equipment for decorating with icings. Look for a set with a plain nozzle and various star nozzles for piping swirls round cupcakes. The larger the star nozzle, the wider the swirls will be on the finished cake. Disposable paper or clear plastic icing bags are available, but nylon piping bags can be washed out in warm soapy water and dried out, ready to re-use again and again.

To Make a Paper Icing Bag

Cut out a 38 x 25.5 cm/15 x 10 inch rectangle of greaseproof paper. Fold it diagonally in half to form two triangular shapes. Cut along the fold line to make two triangles. One of these triangles can be used another time – it is quicker and easier to make two at a time from one square than to measure and mark out a triangle on a sheet of paper.

Fold one of the points on the long side of the triangle over the top to make a sharp cone and hold in the centre. Fold the other sharp end of the triangle over the cone.

Hold all the points together at the back of the cone, keeping the pointed end sharp. Turn the points inside the top edge, fold over to make a crease, then secure with a piece of sticky tape.

To use, snip away the end, place a piping nozzle in position and fill the bag with icing, or fill the bag with icing first, then snip away a tiny hole at the end for piping a plain edge, writing or piping tiny dots.

Ingredients

In baking, most cakes are made by mixing sugar, fats, flour and eggs together. During the mixing, air is incorporated into the mixture to greater or lesser degrees to make it rise during baking. As a cake mixture bakes, the strands of gluten in the flour are stretched and the heat hardens them to give a light sponge-like texture.

Sugar

Sugar is not just included to give sweetness to cakes, it also produces a structure and texture that make a cake tender, so always choose the correct type for your recipe.

Granulated Sugar

This is the standard sugar that you add to your tea. It comes in white and golden unrefined varieties and is used for toppings. The coarseness of granulated sugar means that it does not dissolve easily and is not designed for most baking recipes, so is no good for the creaming method.

Caster Sugar

This is a fine-ground granulated sugar, which also comes in white and golden (or 'natural') unrefined varieties. It blends easily with butter and margarine when beaten or 'creamed' into light sponge mixtures.

Soft Light and Dark Brown Sugars

These cream well and are usually used in richer cakes or spicy fruit mixtures such as carrot cake, and in recipes where rich colour and flavour are needed. Store this sugar in a tightly sealed container to prevent it from drying out. If it does become dry or lumpy, pound it back into crystals with the flat end of a rolling pin before you use it.

Muscovado

This sugar is natural and unrefined, with a deep brown colour and rich flavour that makes fruit cakes and gingerbreads extra special. It comes in light and dark varieties.

Demerara Sugar

Demerara sugar is golden in colour and has a lumpy, grainy texture. It is too coarse for creaming, but is often used for recipes where sugar is melted or as a sparkly topping.

Golden Syrup, Honey, Treacle and Molasses

These are thick liquid sugars. They can be used in cakes made by the melting method but, as they tend to burn at high temperatures, these cakes need to be cooked on a lower heat.

budget (but do not forget the welfare issues involved in this choice). Also, do remember that these may be ungraded and of different sizes, so, for best results, buy eggs marked as 'medium' and 'large'. If you do use economy eggs, make sure to note the sizes you are using and try to even out the quantity by, say, using 1 large and 2 small eggs instead of 3 medium-sized ones.

Egg Powder

Dried egg-white powder gives good results and can be substituted in royal icing recipes, or in recipes where you are unsure about using raw egg whites in the case of the very young, pregnant women or the elderly.

Separating Eggs

When separating whites from their yolks, break them into a cup one at a time so that, if there are any specs of yolk or pieces of shell in the cup, you can easily remove them. If yolk is present in a bowl of whites, it will prevent whisking – even a tiny spec of yolk will stop the whites from whisking into foam and you will have wasted the mixture.

Eggs

Storing

Always store eggs in the refrigerator, but remove them an hour or so before you start to bake, as better results will be achieved if you allow them to reach room temperature before using. This is because, at this temperature, eggs will whisk better and achieve more aeration. This not only gives more volume to the mixture, but also allows the eggs to blend in more easily. Cold eggs used straight from the refrigerator can curdle or split a mixture.

Egg Types

Eggs sold as 'value' or 'economy' can be used for baking cupcakes and muffins, particularly if you are working to a

Yogurt

Plain yogurt is great for adding to sweet and savoury muffins, as it adds richness and moisture to smaller cakes. Do not use low-fat yogurt – stick to plain, thickset natural yogurts that have more substance to them.

Buttermilk

Buttermilk is produced by adding bacteria to low-fat milk to thicken and sour it. This is used in recipes for small cakes and muffins that use bicarbonate of soda, as the acidity from the buttermilk produces carbon dioxide, which raises the cakes. Buttermilk will give an extra lift to cupcakes and muffins, as well as a richer flavour. You will find buttermilk on sale in the dairy section of larger supermarkets but, if it is not available, use 1 tbsp lemon juice to 300 ml/10 fl oz plain yogurt or whole milk as a substitute.

Flours

Plain white flour provides the structure of a cake, but contains nothing to make a cake rise, so cakes that do not need raising agents are made with plain flour. Most recipes using plain flour have bicarbonate of soda or baking powder added to them to make the cakes rise. It is always advisable to sift this into the mixture to incorporate the raising agents evenly.

Self-raising Flour

This has raising agents already added, that will add air to make a cake rise, so is used for light sponge mixtures. If you have only plain flour available, add 2½ tsp baking powder to 225 g/8 oz plain flour to make it into a self-raising flour.

Wholemeal Flour

Wholemeal (sometimes 'wholewheat', or 'brown') flours contain bran from the wheat. This gives a good texture with extra fibre, it tends to keep cupcakes and muffins moist and it gives a mellow flavour. If you want to substitute brown flour for white in a recipe, you will need to add extra liquid, as the bran in brown flour will absorb more fluid (hence why the cakes are more moist).

Storing Flour

White flours should be stored in a cool dry place for up to six months, but wholemeal flours will not keep as long, as they have a higher fat content. So check the use-by date on all packs. Flour is best stored in a sealed airtight container. Always wash and dry this thoroughly before refilling and never add new flour to old. Small micro-organisms will form in very old flour, from the protein, and these can be seen as tiny black specs that will spread into new flour. If you do not have a container, store the opened paper bag inside a large plastic bag and make sure all flour is kept dry. Damp flour weighs more and therefore alters the recipe, which could lead to heavy or flat cakes.

Raising Agents

Raising agents are added to flour to make cakes rise and produce a light texture. It is important to be accurate when measuring these fine powders out, so always use a measuring spoon.

Baking Powder

This is a mixture of bicarbonate of soda and cream of tartar. When liquid is added, the powder fizzes and bubbles and produces carbon dioxide, which expands with heat during baking and gives an airy texture. Be careful not to use very hot or boiling liquid in mixtures, as these can reduce the power of baking powder.

Bicarbonate of Soda or Baking Soda

This is a gentler raising agent and is often used to give melted or spicy mixtures a lift. Cakes will have a bitter flavour if too much is added, so measure this out carefully and accurately with a proper measuring spoon, not a domestic teaspoon.

Fats

Fat adds structure, texture and flavour to cakes and improves their keeping qualities. Always remove them from the refrigerator before using them – they are easier to mix in when at room temperature.

Butter and Hard Block Margarine

Butter and hard margarine can be interchanged in a recipe, and the results will be the same. Butter, however, will always give a better flavour to cupcakes and so, if they are for a special occasion, is it well worth spending a little extra on this.

Soft Margarine

Sold in tubs, this is wonderful for using in all-in-one sponge recipes where all the ingredients are quickly mixed together in one bowl. This fat always produces good results and is quick and easy to use because it does not have to be used at room temperature but can be taken straight from the refrigerator. Do not substitute soft margarine for butter or

hard block margarine in a recipe, as it is a totally different kind of fat, which will not produce the same results. Cupcakes using soft margarine usually require extra raising agent, so do follow the recipe carefully and do not be tempted to over-beat the mixture, as it will become wet and the cakes may sink. Up to 2 minutes' whisking with an electric mixer is fine to make a smooth mixture.

Oils

Oils are useful for muffins and moist cakes such as carrot cake. Use clear light oils such as sunflower or vegetable oil; never use heavy or dark oil. As oils do not hold air, the mixture cannot be creamed, so these cakes will have a denser but beautifully moist texture.

Dried Fruits

Dried Vine Fruits

Fruits such as raisins, currants, sultanas and cranberries (pictured below) are usually sold ready-washed and prepared

for baking, but it is still worth looking through them for pieces of stalk and grit before baking. Dried cranberries, sometimes sold as 'craisins', add a sweet, fresh flavour to cakes, similar to dried cherries. As they are bright red in colour, these can be used as a topping or decoration, as well as baked into mixtures. Fresh cranberries also make a colourful cake decoration.

Glacé Cherries

Sold thinly coated in syrup, these come in a dark maroon natural colour and a brighter red colour (pictured above), the latter usually being cheaper than the natural variety. These cherries keep well stored in their tubs in a cool place. Always wash the syrup off the cherries before baking, as it will cause the cherries to sink in the mixture.

Cherries

These are semi-sweet and are about the size of sultanas. Dried morello cherries have a bittersweet flavour and are delicious added to cupcake recipes.

over cakes to provide a pretty, colourful topping. It needs to be rinsed and dried before use to wash away the sugary coating to reveal the bright green colour. Store it tightly wrapped in a plastic bag inside a sealed container to keep it fresh and flexible.

Ginger

Ginger comes in a sticky glacé variety or in a dried crystallised form (pictured above), coated in sugar crystals. Use both varieties chopped and added to recipes or chop and use with a drizzle icing for an attractive cake topping.

Angelica

A bright green crystallised stem from a herb, this can be chopped into pieces and added to mixtures or scattered

Citrus Peels

Bright and colourful, these add a zesty tang to recipes. Dried orange, lemon and lime peels can be bought as whole large pieces (pictured above) in syrup or a sugar glaze, or ready chopped into small pieces coated in light syrup in a tub (often sold as 'mixed peel'). Keep both varieties in a cool place to prevent crystallisation or drying out of the fruit.

Dried Pineapple

Pineapple for baking comes in many varieties. Soft dried pineapple (pictured below) is sold in thin delicate slices or fans in vacuum-sealed packs and has an intense concentrated flavour, so only use small amounts, chopped into mixtures. These delicate fans make a pretty topping for individual muffins. Keep stored in an airtight container, as the fruits tend to soften once the packs are opened. Use drained canned pineapple rings or chunks for chopping and adding to cake mixtures.

Dried Banana

Dried banana chips (pictured above) make pretty cake toppings for muffins and semi-dried or soft banana chips can be chopped and added to cake mixtures.

Dried Apricots

Dried apricots are richer and sweeter than the fresh fruits. Some dried apricots are shrivelled and have a dark brown colour and these need soaking before use. Look for packs of the ready-to-eat varieties (pictured left), which are soft and moist and ready to use for baking. Organic dried apricots usually have a brighter orange colour and a better flavour, so are worth looking out for.

Dried Coconut

Coconut comes in many varieties. Powdery desiccated coconut comes in fine and sweetened varieties and can be used in mixtures for natural sweetness or as an attractive coating or topping for cupcakes. Dried coconut slices (pictured above) are large sweet wedges, which make a stunning cake topping, or smaller thin-cut coconut chips, which come in natural or toasted varieties, make a great topping pressed into white buttercream.

Prunes

Prunes are dried plums, which add sweetness and richness to baking. Look for packs of ready-to-eat pitted prunes (pictured below), which means they have the stones removed and are ready for chopping.

Dried Figs

Figs are sold as dried, which need to be soaked overnight in hot water, or ready-to-eat (pictured left), and these are plump and moist and ideal for chopping and adding to mixtures.

natural sweetness and flavour or used as decorative toppings. Cupcakes topped with fresh fruits will need to be refrigerated and eaten on the day of decorating.

Spices

Most dried spices have a reasonably long shelf life but will not keep indefinitely, and remember that they will gradually lose their aroma and flavour. It is a good idea to buy in small quantities only when you need them. You will find that both light and heat affect the power and flavour of spices, so, if stored in clear glass jars, keep them out of the light – the best place to store spices is in a dark, cool, dry place.

Dried Dates

Dates are sold in dried blocks, which need to be soaked in warm water before use, or semi-dried or soft ready-to-eat dates (pictured above), which can be used straight away for adding sweetness to mixtures. Remove any stones and use a wetted knife to make chopping the sticky dates easy.

Fresh Fruits

Fresh fruits, such as bananas, citrus fruits and berries, all make great additions to muffin and cupcake recipes. They can be baked into the mixtures for

Nuts

Using nuts in baking is more expensive so, since they deteriorate quickly, it is especially important not to buy them in large quantities. If you buy a large bargain pack of nuts that you are not going to use immediately, store the extra ones in the freezer, where they will keep for up to 6 months. The flavour of nuts, particularly hazelnuts, is always improved by toasting for a few minutes before use. The easiest way to do this is to place them in a single layer on a foil-lined baking tray and grill them lightly.

Almonds

Almonds can be bought in whole, blanched, flaked (above, top), chopped (above, right) or ground (above, left) varieties. Shelled almonds will still have their skins on, so, to remove these, immerse the nuts in boiling water for 2–3 minutes, then plunge into cold water and the skins will slip away easily. Ground almonds have a powdery texture and can be added straight into mixtures to give structure and moistness to a recipe. If you do not have ground almonds available, place whole or flaked almonds in a food processor and grind to a coarse powder. Be careful not to over-grind, however, as too fine a powder will release the natural oils from the nuts.

Hazelnuts

Hazelnuts are sold as whole, skinned or unskinned and ground. For the best flavour in cakes, choose whole skinned nuts and quickly toast them under a grill, then rub away the skins. Chop or grind and use these immediately.

Pecans

Pecan nuts (pictured above) are sweet and richly flavoured, with a superior flavour, but tend to be more expensive than other nuts. One whole nut or a few chopped pieces make an ideal luxury topping for a muffin.

Walnuts

Since walnuts (pictured above) contain more oil than other nuts, they will turn rancid quickly, so do not buy these in bulk. Packs of whole nuts or halves are far more expensive, so, if you need chopped walnuts in a cupcake recipe, buy the cheaper packs sold as walnut pieces, which are equally good.

Peanuts

Peanuts (pictured above) can be used, coarsely chopped, for mixing into muffins and as a crunchy topping for mixtures. Choose ordinary salted peanuts, sold in foil bags, which have the best flavour for recipes.

Flavourings

Flavouring extracts are very concentrated and usually sold in liquid form in small bottles. A teaspoon measure will usually be enough to flavour a cake mixture for 12 muffins. Vanilla and almond extracts are ideal to impart their delicate flavours into cake mixtures and you will find the more expensive extracts give a finer and more natural flavour. Rosewater can be used for flavouring both cake mixtures and icings and has a delicate, perfumed flavour. Fruit flavourings, such as lemon, lime, orange and raspberry, will give a fresh twist to mixtures and icings.

Chocolate

For the best results and a professional finish and flavour, it is always advisable to buy the highest quality chocolate you can find, although this will be more expensive. Better quality chocolates contain a higher percentage of real cocoa fat, which gives a flavour and texture far superior to cheaper varieties. (Cheaper chocolate labelled as 'cooking' or 'baking' chocolate contains a much smaller percentage of cocoa solids and is best avoided in favour of better-quality eating chocolate.) The amount of cocoa fat or solids contained in chocolate will be marked on the wrapper of any good-quality chocolate. Those marked as 70-per-cent cocoa solids will give the best results and you will find this chocolate is shiny and brittle and it should snap very easily.

Dark Chocolate

Also known as 'plain' or 'plain dark' chocolate, this is the most useful all-purpose type of chocolate for baking, as it has a good strong flavour.

Milk Chocolate

Milk chocolate has sugar added and is sweeter than dark, so is good for melting for icings and decorations.

White Chocolate

This is not strictly chocolate, as it contains only cocoa butter, milk and sugar. It is expensive and the most difficult to work with, so must be used with care. It is best to grate it finely and keep the temperature very low when melting it.

Chocolate Cake Covering

This is a cheaper substitute containing a minimum of 2.5-per-cent cocoa solids and vegetable oil. It is considerably cheaper than real chocolate and the flavour is not so good, but it is easy to melt and sets quickly and well for a coating.

Chocolate Chips

Chips come in dark, milk and white varieties and are sold in small bags. They are useful for adding to cupcake and muffin mixtures to enrich them and add a delicious texture as they part melt into the cakes on baking.

Cocoa Powder

Cocoa powder needs to be cooked to release the full flavour, so blend it with boiling water to make into a paste, then cool, before adding to a recipe, or sift it into the bowl with the flour.

Drinking Chocolate

Be aware that this is not the same as cocoa, as it contains milk powder and sugar. Some recipes may specify using drinking chocolate and these are successful, but do not substitute it for cocoa powder, as it will spoil the flavour of a cake.

For Decorating

Icing Sugar

Icing sugar is fine and powdery. It is usually sold plain and white, but can also be bought as an unrefined golden (or 'natural') variety. Use it for delicate icings, frostings and decorations. Store this sugar in a dry place, as it can absorb moisture and this will make it go hard and lumpy. Always sift this sugar at least once, or preferably twice, before you use it, to remove any hard lumps that would prevent icing from achieving a smooth texture – lumpy icing is impossible to pipe out.

Fondant Icing Sugar

This is sold in plain and flavoured varieties and gives a beautiful glossy finish to cake toppings. Just add a little boiled water to the sugar, according to the packet instructions, to make a shiny icing that can be poured or drizzled over cupcake tops to give a very professional finish. Colour the plain white icing with a few spots of paste food colour to achieve your desired result.

Flavoured fondant icing sugar is sold in strawberry, raspberry, orange, lemon and blackcurrant flavours and also has colouring added. These sugars are ideal if you want to make a large batch of cakes with different coloured and flavoured toppings. Flavoured fondant sugars can also be whisked with softened unsalted butter and cream cheese to make delicious frostings in just a few moments.

Royal Icing Sugar

Royal icing sets to a classic, firm Christmas-cake-style covering. Sold in packs as plain white sugar, this is whisked with cold water to give an instant royal icing. It has dried egg white included in the mixture, so does not need the long beating that traditional royal icing recipes require. It is also ideal to use for those who cannot eat raw egg whites.

Tubes of Writing Icing

You can buy small tubes of ready-coloured royal icing or gel icing, usually in sets of black, red, yellow and blue, and these are ideal for small amounts of writing or for piping on dots or small decorations.

Food Colourings

You can buy food colourings in liquid, paste, gel and powder or dust forms in a great range of colours.

Paste food colours are best for using with sugarpaste. These are sold in small tubs and are very concentrated, so should be added to the sugarpaste dot by dot on the end of a wooden cocktail stick. Knead the colouring in evenly, adding more until you get the colour you require.

Liquid and gel food colourings are ideal for adding to frostings. Add this cautiously drop by drop, beating the frosting well until you reach the colour you require.

Dusts and sparkle colourings should be lightly brushed onto dry sugarpaste to form a delicate sheen to decorations such as flowers.

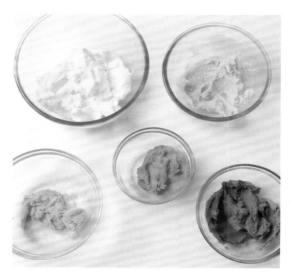

Bought Sugar Decorations and Sprinkles

A selection of pretty sprinkles can be bought in supermarkets or by mail order from specialist cake decorating companies, and these provide a wonderful way to make quick and easy cake toppings.

Basic Techniques

Preparing Tins

Preparing Tins

When recipes give instructions on how to prepare and line tins, these are important steps, so do not be tempted to skimp on these. The time and expense in baking muffins may be wasted if they will not turn out of the tin properly. (*See* pages 20–21.)

Different Making Methods

Creaming

Light cakes are made by the creaming method, which means that the butter and sugar are first beaten or 'creamed' together. A little care is needed for this method. Use a large mixing bowl to beat the fat and sugar together until pale and fluffy. The eggs are gradually beaten in to form a slackened batter and the flour is folded in last, to stiffen up the mixture. In some recipes, egg whites are whisked and added to the mixture separately for extra lightness. When the eggs are added, they are best used at room temperature to prevent the mixture from splitting or 'curdling'. Adding a teaspoon of flour with each beaten egg will help to keep the mixture light and smooth and prevent the mixture from separating. A badly mixed, curdled batter will hold less air and be heavy or can cause a sunken cake.

Rubbing In

In this method, the fat is lightly worked into the flour between the fingers, as in pastry making, until the mixture resembles fine crumbs. This can be done by hand or in a food processor. Enough liquid is stirred in to give a soft mixture that will drop easily from a spoon. This method is used for easy fruit cakes and small buns such as rock cakes.

All-In-One Mixtures

This 'one stage' method is quick and easy and is perfect for those new to baking, as it does not involve any complicated techniques. It is ideal for making light sponges, but soft tub-type margarine or softened butter at room temperature must be used. There is no need for any creaming or rubbing in, as all the ingredients are simply placed in a large bowl and quickly beaten together for just a few minutes until smooth. Be careful not to over-beat, as this will make the mixture too wet. Self-raising flour with the addition of a little extra baking powder is vital for a good rise.

The Melting Method

Cakes with a delicious moist, sticky texture, such as gingerbread, are made by this method. These cakes use a high proportion of sugar and syrup, which are gently warmed together in a saucepan with the fat, until the sugar granules have dissolved and the mixture is liquid. It is important to cool the hot melted mixture a little before beating in flour, eggs and spices to make a batter, otherwise it will damage the power of the raising agent. Bicarbonate of soda is often used as a raising agent in this method, to help raise a heavy batter. These cakes benefit from storing for at least a day before cutting, to make them moist and sticky.

Fruit Cakes

Rich fruit cakes are usually made by the creaming method, then dried fruits and nuts are folded in to the mixture last.

Checking to See if the Cakes Are Cooked

Small cupcakes and muffins should be golden, risen and firm to the touch when pressed lightly in the centre. The last part of a cupcake or muffin to cook is the centre, so, after the baking time stated, check this area. For light sponge-type cakes, press the centre lightly with the fingertips and, if the cake is cooked, it should spring back easily. To test more thoroughly, insert a thin warmed skewer into the deepest part of the centre. If the ,cake is cooked it will come out perfectly cleanly with no mixture sticking to it but, if there is some on the skewer, bake the cakes for a little longer and test again.

Once They're Done

Cooling The Cakes

All freshly baked cakes are very fragile; they need time to stand in the tins to cool for a short time to make them firm.

• Sponges and delicate cupcakes need standing time of about 2 minutes, muffins need 3–4 minutes and fruity mixtures need 5 minutes.

• If muffins start to stick to their moulds, leave until the cakes are firm, then loosen their sides by running round the tins with a small palette knife. Carefully turn the cakes out on a wire rack to cool.

• Do not leave cupcakes in paper cases in the bun trays to cool completely, as moisture that collects in the bun trays will cause the paper cases to go damp and discolour.

What Went Wrong and Why?

Why Did They Sink?

It is important to weigh and measure all the ingredients correctly. If you add too much raising agent, such as baking powder or bicarbonate of soda, this can make the cakes sink. Or cakes can sink in the middle if the mixture was too wet, which can be caused by over-beating when using soft margarine or adding too much liquid. Or opening or slamming the oven door during the baking time can also cause a cake to sink.

Why Has it Not Cooked Fully?

The use of the correct size of tin is important; if the tin is too small, the mixture will not cook through properly. This will also happen if the oven is too cool and the cake is under-baked.

What Caused a Heavy Texture?

The reason for this is usually using too little raising agent, but small cakes can also be close and heavy by adding too much fat, egg or flour. If the mixture is too dry or too wet, it will affect the texture, as will under-mixing – that is, if the cake is not beaten sufficiently to add air, the texture will be coarse.

What Caused a Dry Texture?

Small cakes with a dry texture tend to be crumbly when cut and go stale rapidly. This can be caused if the cakes were baked too slowly or contain too much raising agent. Or the mixture may be too dry if not rubbed in or beaten sufficiently.

What Caused a Crack or Peak in the Top of the Cake?

If the tins contain too much mixture, the batter will rise up and the top will form a peak. Baking in an oven that is too hot or baking the cake too near the heat at the top of the oven will also cause this to happen. A mixture that is too wet or too dry will also form a cracked surface.

What Causes a Dark Hard Outer Crust?

Small cakes with a hard dark outer crust are usually baked in too hot an oven or over-baked in a fan-assisted oven at a high temperature. If you are using a fan-assisted oven, you will usually need to turn the temperature down by 20 degrees or follow your instruction booklet.

Why Did the Fruit Sink?

All vine fruits must be dry when added to the mixture. Glacé cherries must be washed of their syrup, dried and tossed in flour to prevent sinking. If the mixture is too wet or contains too much raising agent, the fruit will sink. Using too cool an oven or opening the oven door too soon before the end of the baking time can cause fruit to sink.

Why Do Cakes Stick to the Pans?

You will not be able to turn the cakes out of a muffin tray if it was not greased sufficiently into all the corners. Cheap or poor-quality tins tend to produce bad results and can buckle in the heat, causing misshapen cakes.

Why Do Small Cakes Spread?

Small cakes spread out if the mixture is too wet or there is too much mixture in each case. Adding too much or too little raising agent will also cause small cakes to flatten out, as will baking in too cool an oven.

Why Are There Large Air Bubbles in the Centre of the Cakes?

Holes in cakes or an uneven texture is caused by under-mixing when adding the flour or liquid. Or if the mixture is too dry, it will tend to contain pockets of air. If the flour and raising agent are not sieved in or properly mixed together, this can also cause air bubbles in the mixture.

Why Did the Cakes Not Rise?

This is caused by not adding enough raising agent or over-beating a mixture and knocking out the air. Or if a mixture is too stiff and does not contain enough liquid, or is baked in too cool an oven, this will not help the cakes rise.

Why Do the Paper Cases Have Brown Marks?

Be careful when filling the paper cases with cake batter, as, if you spill the mixture onto the edges or outsides of the cases, it will cook and burn into dark brown marks that cannot be removed.

How to Patch Up Mistakes

- If your cakes have peaked, then these can easily be trimmed flat when the cakes are cold (see below).

- If the cakes have overcooked or are burnt on the outside, simply scrape this away with a serrated knife and cover the surface with buttercream.

- If the cakes are a little dry, sprinkle them with a few drops of sweet sherry or orange juice.

Cutting the Tops Level

Many cupcakes will form a small peak while baking and this is an ideal shape for coating with buttercream or piping round a swirl of cream cheese icing. However, some methods of decorating cakes require a flat surface, so, for these, trim the tops level with a sharp knife. Coat the cakes with apricot glaze and press on a disc of almond paste or sugarpaste to give you a flat surface to decorate.

Storing Cupcakes and Muffins

- Make sure cakes are completely cold before storing, otherwise condensation can form in the container and this can cause the cakes to go mouldy.

- Large, flat plastic food containers are ideal for cupcakes and muffins, as they enable the cakes to be kept flat in one single layer and will keep small cakes moist. Old-fashioned cake tins can be used, but they do not hold a large number of small cakes.

- If you do not have a large cake container, invert a large mixing bowl over the cakes on a plate or flat surface and the cakes will stay fresh.

- Sponge fairy cakes will keep for 3–4 days, and richer fruit cakes for 5 days to a week.

- Cakes with fresh cream fillings and decorations need to be kept in the refrigerator and are best eaten on the day of filling with cream.

- Savoury muffins are best eaten warm on the day of baking, although they can be reheated or toasted (*see* page 58). Sweet muffins are best eaten on the day of baking and are delicious served warm, but the richer ones will keep for 1–2 days.

- Store cakes with sugarpaste decorations in a cool place, but not in the refrigerator. The moisture in a refrigerator will be absorbed by the sugarpaste and make this icing go limp and soggy.

Transporting

To carry cupcakes to a special event, you will need to use a large flat plastic lidded box. These are ideal and you will find the best boxes are those that stack into each other for ease of carrying. Special cupcake carrying sets are now on sale with a divided base that holds 12 cakes, with raised discs that the cupcakes can sit in, so that they do not move around. A plastic lid with a handle makes these boxes easy to carry. If you do not have special plastic boxes or carriers, replace the cakes in the baking trays to protect them, especially if they are decorated, and place the tins in shallow cardboard boxes for transportation.

Freezing Cupcakes

Most cupcakes will freeze well but, for best results, freeze undecorated. Completely cool each cake and freeze in one layer on a baking sheet or flat tray. Once frozen, place in strong freezer bags or boxes and seal to exclude as much air as possible, label and freeze.

Sweet muffins containing fresh fruits such as blueberries or raspberries will not freeze well, as the fruit tends to make the cakes soggy when thawed, so these are best eaten fresh on the day of baking. If you have any leftover savoury muffins, freeze them in airtight containers or plastic bags and they should keep for up to 2 months.

Thawing and Warming

To use frozen cakes, completely unwrap and thaw at room temperature on racks. The paper cases may peel away from frozen cakes, so these may need to be replaced with fresh ones before decorating the cakes.

To warm savoury muffins, thaw thoroughly or defrost in the microwave. Place on a tray and bake in a preheated oven at 180°C/350°F/Gas Mark 4 for 10 minutes. If you have just a few muffins, these can be thawed, split open and toasted.

Key Cake Recipes

Basic Vanilla Cupcakes

**Makes 18 deep cupcakes, 24 fairy cakes
or 36 mini muffins**

225 g/8 oz butter, softened
    at room temperature
225 g/8 oz caster sugar
4 medium eggs, beaten
225 g/8 oz self-raising flour
½ tsp baking powder
2 tbsp semi-skimmed milk
1 tsp vanilla extract
1 tsp glycerine

Preheat the oven to 180°C/
350°F/Gas Mark 4 and line
appropriate trays with
enough paper cases.

Whisk the butter and
sugar together, preferably
with an electric hand
mixer, until pale and fluffy.
Whisk in the egg gradually,
adding a teaspoon of
flour with each addition
to prevent the mixture
from curdling.

Sift the remaining flour and baking powder into the bowl, then
gradually whisk in the milk, extract and glycerine. Spoon the
mixture into the paper cases and bake for 25 minutes for the
larger cakes, 15 minutes for the fairy cakes or 12 minutes for
the mini muffins, or until firm and golden. Cool on a wire
rack. Keep for 3–4 days in an airtight container.

Mini Cupcakes

Makes about 24

100 g/3½ oz golden caster sugar
100 g/3½ oz butter, softened
finely grated zest and juice of ½ lemon
2 medium eggs, beaten
100 g/3½ oz self-raising flour
2 tsp milk

Preheat the oven to 190°C/
375°F/Gas Mark 5. Grease a
mini-muffin tray or line it with
mini paper cases.

Put the sugar, butter and
lemon zest in a large bowl
and beat until light and
fluffy. Add the beaten egg
a little at a time, with a
teaspoon of flour with each
addition. Fold in the flour
and lemon juice and mix
until smooth.

Spoon into the mini-muffin tray or cases and bake for about
12 minutes until golden and risen. Transfer to a rack
to cool. Keep for 2–3 days in an airtight container.

Quick All-in-One Mix for Cupcakes

Makes 12 deep cupcakes or 18 fairy cakes

125 g/4 oz caster sugar
125 g/4 oz soft-tub margarine
2 medium eggs
125 g/4 oz self-raising flour
1 tsp milk or lemon juice

Preheat the oven to 190°C/375°F/Gas Mark 5. Line appropriate trays with enough paper cases for the cakes.

Place all the cake ingredients in a large bowl and beat with an electric mixer for about 2 minutes until smooth. Half-fill the paper cases with the mixture.

Bake for about 15 minutes until firm, risen and golden. Remove to a wire rack to cool. Keep for 2–3 days in an airtight container.

Individual Fruit Cakes

Makes 18 fairy cakes

125 g/4 oz butter
125 g/4 oz soft dark muscovado sugar
2 medium eggs, beaten
225 g/8 oz self-raising flour
1 tsp ground mixed spice
finely grated zest, and 1 tbsp juice,
    of 1 orange
1 tbsp black treacle
350 g/12 oz mixed dried fruit

Preheat the oven to 180°C/350°F/Gas Mark 4. Line a fairy-cake muffin tray with paper cases.

Beat the butter and sugar together until light and fluffy, then beat in the eggs a little at a time, adding a teaspoon of flour with each addition. Sift in the remaining flour and spice, add the orange zest and juice, treacle and dried fruit to the bowl and fold together until the mixture is blended.

Spoon into the tins and bake for 30 minutes until firm in the centre and a skewer comes out clean. Leave to cool in the tins for 15 minutes, then turn out to cool on a wire rack. Store in an airtight container for up to 4 weeks or freeze until needed.

Chocolate Fudge Cakes

Makes 12 deep cupcakes, 18 cupcakes
or 22 mini cupcakes

150 g/5 oz butter, softened
150 g/5 oz golden caster sugar
3 medium eggs, beaten
125 g/4 oz self-raising flour
25 g/1 oz cocoa powder
1 tbsp milk

Preheat the oven to
190°C/375°F/Gas Mark 5.
Line appropriate trays with
enough foil or paper cake
cases.

Place the butter, caster
sugar and eggs in a large
bowl and then sift in the
flour and cocoa powder.
Whisk together with the
milk until smooth for about
2 minutes, then spoon into
the cases, filling them two-
thirds full.

Bake for about 20 minutes for the deep cakes, 14 minutes
for the cupcakes or 12–14 minutes for the mini cupcakes
until well risen and springy to the touch. Cool on a wire rack.
Keep for 3 days in an airtight container.

Carrot Cupcakes

Makes 12 deep cupcakes, 18 cupcakes or 22 mini cupcakes

225 g/8 oz carrots, peeled
175 g/6 oz self-raising wholemeal flour
1 tsp baking powder
½ tsp ground cinnamon
pinch salt
150 ml/¼ pt sunflower oil
150 g/5 oz soft light brown sugar
3 medium eggs, beaten
1 tsp vanilla extract
50 g/2 oz sultanas or raisins

Preheat the oven to 180°C/350°F/Gas Mark 4. Lightly oil or line appropriate trays with enough paper cases for the cakes. Grate the carrots finely.

Sift the flour, baking powder, cinnamon and salt into a bowl, then tip in any bran from the sieve. Add the oil, sugar, eggs, extract, sultanas and grated carrots.

Beat until smooth, then spoon into the muffin trays. Bake for 25 minutes for the deep cakes, 20 minutes for the cupcakes or 15–20 minutes for the mini muffins until risen and golden. Cool on a wire rack. Keep for 5 days in an airtight container.

Key Icing Recipes

Cream Cheese Frosting

Covers 12 small cakes

50 g/2 oz unsalted butter, softened at room temperature
300 g/11 oz icing sugar, sifted
flavouring of choice
food colourings of choice
125 g/4 oz full-fat cream cheese

Beat the butter and icing sugar together until light and fluffy.
Add flavourings and colourings of choice and beat again.
Add the cream cheese and whisk until light and fluffy.
Do not over-beat, however, as the mixture can become runny.

Basic Buttercream Frosting

Covers 12 small cakes

150 g/5 oz unsalted butter,
    softened at room temperature
225 g/8 oz icing sugar, sifted
2 tbsp hot milk or water
1 tsp vanilla extract
food colourings of choice

Beat the butter until light and fluffy, then beat
in the sifted icing sugar and hot milk or water in
two batches. Add the vanilla extract and any food
colourings. Store, chilled for up to two days in
 lidded container.

Variations

Omit the vanilla extract and instead:

Coffee Blend 2 tsp coffee extract with the milk.

Chocolate Blend 2 tbsp cocoa powder to a paste
with 2 tbsp boiling water and use instead of the hot
milk or water.

Citrus Add the finely grated zest of 1 small orange,
lemon or lime, plus 1 tbsp orange juice or 2 tsp fresh
lemon or lime juice instead of the milk or water.

Chocolate Fudge Icing

Covers 12 small cakes

125 g/4 oz dark chocolate, broken into pieces
50 g/2 oz unsalted butter
1 medium egg, beaten
175 g/6 oz natural icing sugar, sifted
½ tsp vanilla extract

Place the chocolate and butter in a bowl over a pan of hot water and stir until melted. Remove from the heat and whisk in the egg with the icing sugar and vanilla. Whisk until smooth and glossy, then use immediately or leave to cool and thicken for a spreading consistency.

Royal Icing

Makes 500 g/1 lb 2 oz to cover 12 deep muffins

2 medium egg whites
500 g/1 lb 2 oz icing sugar, sifted
2 tsp lemon juice

Put the egg whites in a large bowl and whisk lightly with a fork to break up the whites until foamy. Sift in half the icing sugar with the lemon juice and beat well with an electric mixer for 4 minutes or by hand with a wooden spoon for about 10 minutes until smooth.

Gradually sift in the remaining icing sugar and beat again until thick, smooth and brilliant white and the icing forms soft peaks when flicked up with a spoon.

Keep the royal icing covered with a clean damp cloth until you are ready to use it, or store in the refrigerator in a tightly lidded plastic container until needed. If making royal icing ahead of time to use later, beat it again before use to remove any air bubbles that may have formed in the mixture.

Tip For a softer royal icing that will not set too hard, beat 1 tsp glycerine into the mixture.

Glacé Icing

Covers 12 small cakes

225 g/8 oz icing sugar
few drops lemon juice or vanilla or almond extract
2–3 tbsp boiling water
liquid food colouring (optional)

Sift the icing sugar into a bowl and add the chosen flavouring. Gradually stir in enough water to mix to a consistency of thick cream. Beat with a wooden spoon until the icing is thick enough to coat the back of the spoon. Add colouring, if liked, and use at once, as the icing will begin to form a skin.

Variations

Citrus Replace the water with freshly squeezed, strained orange or lemon juice.

Chocolate Sift 2 tsp cocoa powder into the icing sugar.

Coffee Dissolve 1 tsp coffee granules in 1 tbsp of the hot water and cool or add 1 tsp liquid coffee extract.

Apricot Glaze

Makes 450 g/1 lb to cover 24 small cakes

450 g/1 lb apricot jam
3 tbsp water
1 tsp lemon juice

Place the jam, water and juice in a heavy-based saucepan and heat gently, stirring, until soft and melted.

Boil rapidly for 1 minute, then press through a fine sieve with the back of a wooden spoon. Discard the pieces of fruit.

Use immediately for glazing or sticking on almond paste, or pour into a clean jar or plastic lidded container and store in the refrigerator for up to 3 months.

Almond Paste

Makes 450 g/1 lb to cover 24 small cakes

125 g/4 oz sifted icing sugar
125 g/4 oz caster sugar
225 g/8 oz ground almonds
1 medium egg
1 tsp lemon juice

Stir the sugars and ground almonds together in a bowl. Whisk the egg and lemon juice together and mix into the dry ingredients.

Knead until the paste is smooth. Wrap tightly in clingfilm or foil to keep airtight and store in the refrigerator until needed. The paste can be made 2–3 days ahead of time but, after that, it will start to dry out and become difficult to handle.

To use the almond paste, knead on a surface lightly dusted with icing sugar until soft and pliable. Brush the top of each cake with apricot glaze. Roll out the almond paste and cut out discs large enough to cover the tops of the cakes. Press onto the cakes.

Sugarpaste Icing

**Makes 350 g/12 oz to cover 12 small
cakes or use for decorations**

1 medium egg white
1 tbsp liquid glucose
350 g/12 oz icing sugar, sifted

Place the egg white and liquid glucose
in a large mixing bowl and stir together
with a fork, breaking up the egg white.
Add the icing sugar gradually, mixing in
with a palette knife until the mixture
binds together and forms a ball.

Turn the ball of icing out onto a clean surface dusted with
icing sugar and knead for 5 minutes until soft but firm enough
to roll out. If the icing is too soft, knead in a little more icing
sugar until the mixture is pliable.

To colour, knead in paste food colouring. Do not use liquid
food colour, as this is not suitable and will make the
sugarpaste go limp.

To use, roll out thinly on a clean surface dusted with icing
sugar and cut out discs large enough to cover the top of each
cake. Brush the almond paste (if using as a layer underneath
the sugarpaste discs) with a little cold boiled water or a clear

spirit such as kirsch and press onto the cake, then press the
sugarpaste on top of the almond paste topping. Alternatively,
coat the cakes with a little buttercream, place the sugarpaste
disc on top and press down.

To mould, knead lightly and roll out thinly on a surface
dusted with icing sugar. Use cutters or templates (*see* page
79) to make flowers or shapes. Mould into shapes with your
fingertips and leave to dry out for 24 hours in egg boxes
lined with clingfilm.

Decorating

Using Chocolate

Melting Chocolate

Care and attention is needed to melt chocolate for baking and cake decorating needs. If the chocolate gets too hot or comes into contact with water or steam, it will 'seize' or stiffen and form into a hard ball instead of a smooth melted mixture. You can add a little vegetable oil or margarine, a teaspoon at a time, to the mixture to make it liquid again.

To melt chocolate, break the bar into small pieces, or grate or chop it, and place in a heatproof bowl standing over a bowl of warm, not hot, water. Make sure the bowl containing the chocolate is completely dry and that steam or water cannot enter the bowl. Heat the water to a gentle simmer only and leave the bowl to stand for about 5 minutes. Do not let the water get too hot or the chocolate will reach too high a temperature and will lose its sheen.

The microwave oven is ideal for melting chocolate. Place the chocolate pieces in a small microwave-proof bowl and melt gently on low or defrost settings in small bursts of 30 seconds, checking and stirring in between, until the chocolate has melted.

Making Chocolate Decorations

Curls and shavings Spread melted chocolate out thinly onto a clean dry surface such as a plastic board, marble or a clean worktop. Leave the chocolate until almost set, then pull a long sharp-bladed knife through it at an angle to form curls or shavings. Place the curls in a lidded plastic box in the refrigerator until needed for decoration.

Leaves Wash and dry holly or rose leaves and place on a sheet of nonstick baking parchment. Melt the chocolate and paint on the underside of each leaf. Leave to dry out, then carefully peel away the leaf. You will find the veined side is uppermost on the chocolate leaf. Place in a lidded container and keep refrigerated until needed for decoration.

Crystallising Petals, Flowers, Leaves and Berries

Wash and dry herbs and leaves such as rosemary sprigs and small bay leaves or berries such as cranberries. Separate edible petals from small flowers such as rosebuds and clean small flowers such as violets with a clean brush, but do not wash them.

Beat 1 medium egg white with 2 tsp cold water until frothy. Paint a thin layer of egg white carefully over the items, then sprinkle lightly with caster sugar, shaking to remove any excess. Leave to dry on a wire rack lined with nonstick baking parchment.

Using Buttercream and Cream Cheese Frostings

These soft icings can be swirled onto the tops of cupcakes with a small palette knife or placed in a piping bag fitted with a star nozzle to pipe impressive whirls.

- Do not be mean with the amount of frosting you use. If this is scraped on thinly, you will see the cake underneath, so be generous.

- Keep cupcakes with frostings in a cool place, or refrigerate, as they contain a high percentage of butter, which will melt easily in too warm a place.

- Cakes coated in buttercream can be decorated easily with colourful sprinkles and sugars. To make this easy, place the sprinkles in a small saucer or on a piece of nonstick baking parchment and roll the outside edges of each cake in the decorations.

Using Sugarpaste

Sugarpaste is a versatile icing, as it can be used for covering small cakes or modelling all sorts of fancy decorations. To use as a covering, roll out the sugarpaste thinly on a surface dusted with icing sugar and cut out circles the size of the cake tops. Coat each cake with a little apricot glaze or buttercream and press on the circles to form a flat surface.

To Copy Patterns from the Templates

At the back of this book, you will find templates for some of the shapes below and as used in this book. Trace the pattern you want onto a sheet of clear greaseproof paper or nonstick baking parchment. Roll out the sugarpaste thinly, then position the traced pattern. Mark over the pattern with the tip of a small sharp knife or a pin. Remove the paper and cut out the marked-on pattern with a small sharp knife.

Making Flat Decorations

To make letters, numbers or flat decorations, roll out the sugarpaste thinly and cut out the shapes. Leave to dry on nonstick baking parchment on a flat surface or a tray for 2–3 hours to make them firm and easy to handle.

Making Roses

Colour the sugarpaste icing with pink paste food colouring. Take a small piece of sugarpaste and make a small cone shape, then roll a small pea-sized piece of sugarpaste into a ball. Flatten out the ball into a petal shape and wrap this round the cone shape. Continue adding more petals, then trim the thick base. Leave to dry for 2 hours in a clean egg box lined with foil or clingfilm.

Making Lilies

Colour a little sugarpaste a deep yellow and mould this into thin sausage shapes. Leave these to firm on nonstick baking parchment or clingfilm for 2 hours. Thinly roll out white sugarpaste and mark out small squares of 4 x 4 cm/1½ x 1½ inches. Wrap each square round a yellow centre to form a lily and press the end together. Place the lilies on nonstick baking parchment to dry out for 2 hours.

Making Daisies

Roll out a little sugarpaste thinly and, using a daisy stamp cutter (*see* page 234), press out small flower shapes and mould these into a curve. Leave the daisies to dry out on nonstick baking parchment, then pipe dots into the centre of each one with yellow royal icing or a small gel tube of writing icing.

Making Butterfly Wings

Colour the sugarpaste and roll out thinly. Trace round the butterfly patterns and cut out the wing shapes. Leave these to dry, flat, on nonstick baking parchment for 4 hours to make them firm and easy to lift.

Decorating Tips

- Always roll out almond paste or sugarpaste icing on a surface lightly dusted with icing sugar.

- Leave sugarpaste-covered cakes to firm up for 2 hours before adding decorations, as this provides a good finished surface to work on.

- Tie ribbons round the finished cake and secure them with a dab of royal icing. Never use pins in ribbons on a cake.

- Once decorated, store sugarpaste-covered cakes in large boxes in a cool place. Do not store in a refrigerator, as the sugarpaste will become damp and colours may run.

- Paste food colourings are best for working with sugarpaste and a little goes a very long way. As these are very concentrated, use a cocktail stick to add dots of paste gradually, until you are sure of the colour, and knead in until even.

Teatime Treats

MAKES 12 DEEP CUPCAKES OR 18 FAIRY CAKES

Lemon Drizzle Cupcakes

150 g/5 oz butter, softened
150 g/5 oz caster sugar
3 medium eggs, beaten

150 g/5 oz self-raising flour
½ tsp baking powder
1 lemon

To decorate:
1 lemon
50 g/2 oz caster sugar

Preheat the oven to 180°C/350°F/Gas Mark 4 and line a 12-hole muffin tray with paper cases, or two fairy-cake trays with 18 fairy-cake paper cases.

Place the butter, sugar and eggs in a bowl and then sift in the flour and baking powder. Finely grate the zest of the lemon into the bowl.

Beat together for about 2 minutes, preferably with an electric hand mixer, until pale and fluffy. Spoon into the paper cases and bake for 25 minutes for the larger cupcakes and 15 minutes for the fairy cakes until firm and golden. Cool on a wire rack.

To make the topping, cut the zest from the other lemon into thin strips and set aside. Squeeze the juice from the lemon into a small saucepan. Add the sugar and heat gently until every grain of sugar has dissolved. Add the strips of zest and cool slightly. Spoon the syrup and lemon strips over the cupcakes while still warm. Leave to cool. Keep for 4 days in an airtight container.

Mini Carrot Cupcakes

MAKES 22

175 g/6 oz self-raising
   wholemeal flour
1 tsp baking powder
½ tsp ground cinnamon
pinch salt
150 ml/¼ pint sunflower oil

150 g/5 oz soft light
   brown sugar
3 medium eggs, beaten
1 tsp vanilla extract
50 g/2 oz sultanas
225 g/8 oz carrots, peeled
   and grated

To decorate:
1 orange
75 g/3 oz cream cheese
175 g/6 oz golden icing sugar

Preheat the oven to 180°C/350°F/Gas Mark 4. Lightly oil two 12-hole mini-muffin trays.

Sift the flour, baking powder, cinnamon and salt into a bowl, with any bran from the sieve. Add the oil, sugar, eggs, vanilla extract, sultanas and grated carrots.

Beat until smooth, then spoon into the muffin trays. Bake for about 20 minutes until risen and golden. Cool on a wire rack.

To decorate, peel thin strips of zest from the orange. Beat the cream cheese and icing sugar together with 2 tsp juice from the orange to make a spreading consistency. Swirl the icing over each cupcake and then top with shreds of orange zest. Keep for 3 days in an airtight container in a cool place.

Sticky Toffee Cupcakes

MAKES 16–18

50 g/5 oz stoned dates, chopped
1 tsp bicarbonate of soda
225 ml/8 fl oz hot water
175 g/6 oz plain flour
1 tsp baking powder

50 g/2 oz butter or block margarine, diced
200 g/7 oz soft light brown sugar
1 large egg, beaten
½ tsp vanilla extract

For the icing:
25 g/1 oz unsalted butter
5 tbsp soft light brown sugar
4 tbsp double cream

Preheat the oven to 180°C/350°F/Gas Mark 4. Line one or two bun trays with 16–18 fairy-cake cases, depending on the depth of the tray holes. Place the chopped dates in a bowl with the bicarbonate of soda and pour over the hot water. Stir, then set aside to cool.

Sift the flour and baking powder into a bowl and add the diced butter. Rub in between your fingertips until the mixture resembles fine crumbs. Stir in the sugar and mix well. Add the egg, vanilla extract and the date mixture. Beat with a wooden spoon until smooth.

Spoon into the cases and bake for about 25 minutes until well risen and firm to the touch in the centre. Leave to cool in the tins for 5 minutes, then turn out to cool on a wire rack.

To make the topping, place the butter, sugar and cream in a small pan over a low heat and stir until the sugar dissolves. Bring to the boil and boil for 1–2 minutes until the mixture thickens. Brush quickly over each fairy cake, as the mixture will set as it cools. Keep for 2 days in an airtight container.

Shaggy Coconut Cupcakes

MAKES 12

½ tsp baking powder
200 g/7 oz self-raising flour
175 g/6 oz caster sugar
2 tbsp desiccated coconut
175 g/6 oz soft margarine
3 medium eggs, beaten
2 tbsp milk

To decorate:
1 batch buttercream
  (*see* page page 68)
1 tbsp coconut liqueur
  (optional)
175 g/6 oz large shredded
  coconut strands

Preheat the oven to 180°C/350°F/Gas Mark 4. Line a 12-hole deep muffin tray with paper cases.

Sift the baking powder and flour into a large bowl. Add all the remaining ingredients and beat for about 2 minutes until smooth and creamy. Divide evenly between the paper cases.

Bake for 18–20 minutes until risen, golden and firm to the touch. Leave in the muffin trays for 2 minutes, then turn out to cool on a wire rack.

To decorate the cupcakes, if you are using the coconut liqueur, beat this into the buttercream, and then swirl over each cupcake. To decorate, press large strands of shredded coconut into the buttercream. Keep for 3 days in an airtight container in a cool place.

Coffee & Walnut Fudge Cupcakes

MAKES 16–18

125 g/4 oz self-raising flour
125 g/4 oz butter, softened
125 g/ 4 oz golden
   caster sugar
2 medium eggs, beaten
1 tbsp golden syrup

50 g/2 oz walnuts,
   finely chopped

To decorate:
225 g/8 oz golden icing sugar
125 g/4 oz unsalted butter, at

room temperature
2 tsp coffee extract
16–18 small walnut pieces

Preheat the oven to 200°C/400°F/Gas Mark 6. Line two 12-hole bun trays with 16–18 small foil cases, depending on the depth of the tray holes.

Stir the flour into a bowl and add the butter, sugar, eggs and syrup. Beat for about 2 minutes, then fold in the walnuts.

Spoon the mixture into the paper cases and bake for about 12–14 minutes until well risen and springy in the centre. Remove to a wire rack to cool.

Make the frosting by sifting the icing sugar into a bowl. Add the butter, coffee extract and 1 tbsp hot water. Beat until light and fluffy, then place in a piping bag fitted with a star nozzle. Pipe a swirl on each cupcake and top with a walnut piece. Keep for 3–4 days in an airtight container in a cool place.

Madeleine Cupcakes

MAKES 10–12

125 g/4 oz self-raising flour
125 g/4 oz butter, softened
125 g/4 oz golden caster sugar
2 medium eggs, beaten
1 tsp vanilla extract

To decorate:
4 tbsp seedless raspberry jam
65 g/2½ oz desiccated
    coconut
glacé cherries, halved

Preheat the oven to 180°C/350°F/Gas Mark 4. Line a 12-hole muffin tray with 10–12 paper cases, depending on the depth of the holes.

Sift the flour into a bowl and add the butter, sugar, eggs and extract. Beat for about 2 minutes until smooth, then spoon into the paper cases.

Bake in the centre of the oven for about 14–16 minutes until well risen and springy in the centre. Transfer to a wire rack to cool.

To decorate the cupcakes, warm the raspberry jam in a small pan or in the microwave oven in a heatproof dish on low for a few seconds. Brush the warmed jam over the top of each cupcake. Lightly coat the top of each cupcake with coconut, then finish with a halved cherry. Keep for 3 days in an airtight container.

Lamington Cupcakes

MAKES 12

125 g/4 oz self-raising flour
125 g/4 oz butter, softened
125 g/4 oz golden
   caster sugar
2 medium eggs, beaten
1 tsp vanilla extract

To decorate:
350 g/12 oz caster sugar
1 tbsp cocoa powder
125 ml/4 fl oz water
65 g/2½ oz desiccated
   coconut

ready-made chocolate
   decorations

Preheat the oven to 180°C/350°F/Gas Mark 4. Line a 12-hole muffin tray with deep paper cases.

Sift the flour into a bowl and add the butter, sugar, eggs and extract. Beat for about two minutes until smooth, then spoon into the paper cases.

Bake in the centre of the oven for about 18 minutes until well risen and springy in the centre. Transfer to a wire rack to cool.

To make the icing, place the caster sugar, cocoa powder and water in a large heavy-based pan. Heat over a low heat until every grain of sugar has dissolved. Bring to the boil and then simmer for about 6 minutes, without stirring, until thickened into syrup. Pour into a bowl and use the syrup while it is still hot, as it will set as it cools.

Place the coconut into a large bowl. Dip the top of each cupcake into the hot chocolate syrup to coat the top, then dip in coconut, decorate and place on a tray to dry. Keep for 2–3 days in an airtight container.

Mini Cupcakes

MAKES 24

100 g/3½ oz golden
   caster sugar
100 g/3½ oz butter,
   softened
finely grated zest of ½ lemon
   and 1 tsp juice

2 medium eggs, beaten
100 g/3½ oz self-raising flour

To decorate:
50 g/2 oz unsalted
   butter, softened

1 tsp vanilla extract
125 g/4 oz icing sugar, sifted
1 tbsp milk
paste food colours
sugar sprinkles

Preheat the oven to 190°C/375°F/Gas Mark 5. Line a 24-hole mini-muffin tray with mini paper muffin cases.

Put the sugar, butter and lemon zest in a large bowl and beat until light and fluffy. Beat in the egg a little at a time, adding a teaspoon of flour with each addition. Fold in the rest of the flour and the lemon juice and mix until smooth.

Spoon into the mini muffin cases and bake for about 12 minutes until golden and risen. Transfer to a wire rack to cool.

To make the icing, beat the butter and vanilla extract together until light and fluffy, then gradually beat in the icing sugar and milk until a soft, easy-to-spread consistency has formed. Colour the icing in batches with paste food colour, then spread over the cold cupcakes with a flat-bladed knife. Decorate with sugar sprinkles. Keep in an airtight container for 2 days.

Raspberry Butterfly Cupcakes

MAKES 12–14

125 g/4 oz caster sugar
125 g/4 oz soft tub margarine
2 medium eggs

125 g/4 oz self-raising flour
½ tsp baking powder
½ tsp vanilla extract

To decorate:
4 tbsp seedless raspberry jam
12–14 fresh raspberries
icing sugar, to dust

Preheat the oven to 190°C/375°F/Gas Mark 5. Line one or two bun trays with
12–14 paper cases, depending on the depth of the holes.

Place all the cupcake ingredients in a large bowl and beat with an electric mixer for about
2 minutes until smooth. Fill the paper cases halfway up with the mixture.

Bake for about 15 minutes until firm, risen and golden. Remove to a wire rack to cool.
When cold, cut a small circle out of the top of each cupcake and then cut the circle in half
to form wings.

Fill each cupcake with a teaspoon of raspberry jam. Replace the wings at an angle and
top each with a fresh raspberry. Dust lightly with icing sugar and serve immediately.

Strawberry Swirl Cupcakes

MAKES 12

125 g/4 oz caster sugar
125 g/4 oz soft tub margarine
2 medium eggs
125 g/4 oz self-raising flour
½ tsp baking powder
2 tbsp sieved strawberry jam

To decorate:
50 g/2 oz unsalted butter at
    room temperature
300 g/11 oz icing
    sugar, sifted

125 g/4 oz full-fat
    cream cheese
1 tbsp sieved
    strawberry jam
pink food colouring

Preheat the oven to 190°C/375°F/Gas Mark 5. Line a muffin tray with 12 deep paper cases.

Place all the cupcake ingredients except the jam in a large bowl and beat with an electric mixer for about 2 minutes until smooth. Fill the paper cases halfway up with the mixture.

Add ½ teaspoon jam to each case and swirl it into the mixture. Bake for about 15 minutes until firm, risen and golden. Remove to a wire rack to cool.

To prepare the frosting, beat the butter until soft, then gradually add the icing sugar until the mixture is light. Add the cream cheese and whisk until light and fluffy. Divide the mixture in half and beat the strawberry jam and pink food colouring into one half. Fit a piping bag with a wide star nozzle and spoon strawberry cream on one side of the bag and the plain cream on the other. Pipe swirls on top of the cupcakes. Keep for 3 days in an airtight container in a cool place.

**MAKES 12 LARGE
CUPCAKES OR
18 FAIRY CAKES**

Double Cherry Cupcakes

50 g/2 oz glacé
   cherries, washed,
   dried and chopped
125 g/4 oz self-raising flour
25 g/1 oz dried morello
   cherries

125 g/4 oz soft margarine
125 g/4 oz caster sugar
2 medium eggs
½ tsp almond extract

To decorate:
125 g/4 oz fondant
   icing sugar
pale pink liquid food
   colouring
40 g/1½ oz glacé cherries

Preheat the oven to 190°C/375°F/Gas Mark 5. Line a 12-hole muffin tray with deep paper cases, or two trays with 18 fairy-cake cases.

Dust the chopped glacé cherries lightly in a tablespoon of the flour, then mix with the morello cherries and set aside. Sift the rest of the flour into a bowl, then add the margarine, sugar, eggs and almond extract. Beat for about 2 minutes until smooth, then fold in the cherries.

Spoon the batter into the paper cases and bake for 15–20 minutes until well risen and springy in the centre. Turn out to cool on a wire rack.

To decorate the cupcakes, trim the tops level. Mix the icing sugar with 2–3 tsp warm water and a few drops of pink food colouring to make a thick consistency. Spoon the icing over each cupcake filling right up to the edge. Chop the cherries finely and sprinkle over the icing. Leave to set for 30 minutes. Keep for 3 days in an airtight container.

Ginger & Lemon Cupcakes

MAKES 18

8 tbsp golden syrup
125 g/4 oz block margarine
225 g/8 oz plain flour
2 tsp ground ginger
75 g/3 oz sultanas

50 g/2 oz soft dark
    brown sugar
200 ml/7 fl oz milk
1 tsp bicarbonate of soda
1 medium egg, beaten

To decorate:
125 g/4 oz golden icing sugar
1 tsp lemon juice
glacé ginger pieces

Preheat the oven to 180°C/350°F/Gas Mark 4. Line two shallow muffin trays with 18 paper cases.

Place the syrup and margarine in a heavy-based pan and melt together gently. Sift the flour and ginger into a bowl, then stir in the sultanas and sugar. Warm the milk and stir in the bicarbonate of soda.

Pour the syrup mixture, milk and beaten egg into the dry ingredients and beat until smooth. Pour the mixture into a jug.

Carefully spoon 2 tbsp of the mixture into each case (the mixture will be wet). Bake for about 30 minutes. Cool in the tins for 10 minutes, then turn out to cool on a wire rack.

To decorate, blend the icing sugar with the lemon juice and 1 tbsp warm water to make a thin glacé icing. Drizzle over the top of each cupcake, then top with glacé ginger pieces. Leave to set for 30 minutes. Keep in an airtight container for up to 5 days.

Crystallised Violet Cupcakes

MAKES 12

150 g/5 oz butter, softened
150 g/5 oz caster sugar
3 medium eggs, beaten
150 g/5 oz self-raising
   flour

½ tsp baking powder
1 lemon

To decorate:
12 fresh violets

1 egg white
caster sugar
125 g/4 oz fondant icing sugar
pale violet food colouring

Preheat the oven to 180°C/350°F/Gas Mark 4 and line a 12-hole muffin tray with deep paper cases.

Place the butter, sugar and eggs in a bowl. Sift in the flour and baking powder. Finely grate in the zest from the lemon.

Beat together for about 2 minutes with an electric hand mixer until pale and fluffy. Spoon into the paper cases and bake for 20–25 minutes until firm and golden. Cool on a wire rack.

To decorate the cupcakes, spread the violets on some nonstick baking parchment. Beat the egg white until frothy, then brush thinly over the violets. Dust with caster sugar and leave to dry out for 2 hours. Beat the icing sugar with the colouring and enough water to give a thin coating consistency. Drizzle over the top of each cupcake quickly and top with a violet. Leave to set for 30 minutes. Store in an airtight container in a cool place. Keep for 2 days.

Cream Cheese Pastel Swirls

MAKES 12

150 g/5 oz butter, softened
150 g/5 oz caster sugar
175 g/6 oz self-raising flour
3 medium eggs
1 tsp vanilla extract

To decorate:
1 batch cream cheese
    frosting (*see* page 67)
paste food colourings

Preheat the oven to 180°C/350°F/Gas Mark 4. Line a 12-hole muffin tray with deep paper cases.

Place butter and sugar in a bowl and cream together. In another bowl beat the eggs with the vanilla extract. Sift the flour into the creamed mixture then beat in the eggs until smooth. Spoon into the cases, filling them three-quarters full.

Bake for about 18 minutes until firm to the touch in the centre. Turn out to cool on a wire rack.

Divide the frosting into three batches. Colour one green and one pink with dots of food colouring and leave one batch plain. Place each batch in a piping bag fitted with a star nozzle and pipe large swirls on top of each cupcake. Keep for 3 days in an airtight container in a cool place.

Daisy Chain Lemon Cupcakes

MAKES 12

125 g/4 oz caster sugar
125 g/4 oz soft tub margarine
2 medium eggs
125 g/4 oz self-raising flour
½ tsp baking powder
1 tsp lemon juice

To decorate:
50 g/2 oz ready-to-roll
   sugarpaste icing
yellow piping icing tube
225 g/8 oz fondant
   icing sugar

lemon yellow
   food colouring

Preheat the oven to 190°C/375°F/Gas Mark 5. Line a bun tray with 12 paper cases.

Place all the cupcake ingredients in a large bowl and beat with an electric mixer for about 2 minutes until smooth. Fill the paper cases halfway up with the mixture.

Bake for about 15 minutes until firm, risen and golden. Remove to a wire rack to cool.

Roll out the icing thinly and stamp out small daisies with a fluted daisy cutter. Pipe a small yellow dot of icing into the centre of each and leave to dry out for 1 hour. Blend the fondant icing sugar with a little water and a few dots of yellow colouring to make a thick easy-to-spread icing, then smooth over the top of each cupcake. Decorate with the cut-out daisies immediately and leave to set for 1 hour. Keep for 3 days in an airtight container.

Florentine–topped Cupcakes

MAKES 18

150 g/5 oz butter, softened
150 g/5 oz caster sugar
175 g/6 oz self-raising flour
3 medium eggs
1 tsp vanilla extract
75 g/3 oz glacé

cherries, chopped
50 g/2 oz angelica, chopped
50 g/2 oz candied peel,
chopped
50 g/2 oz dried cranberries

To decorate:
75 g/3 oz plain or milk
chocolate, melted
50 g/2 oz flaked almonds

Preheat the oven to 180°C/350°F/Gas Mark 4. Line two 12-hole muffin trays with 18 paper cases.

Place the butter and sugar in a bowl, then sift in the flour. In another bowl, beat the eggs with the vanilla extract, then add to the first mixture and beat until smooth. Fold in half the cherries, angelica, peel and cranberries. Spoon into the cases, filling them three-quarters full.

Bake for about 18 minutes until firm to the touch in the centre. Turn out to cool on a wire rack.

Spoon a little melted chocolate on top of each cupcake, then scatter the remaining cherries, angelica, peel and cranberries and the almonds into the wet chocolate. Drizzle the remaining chocolate over the fruit topping with a teaspoon and leave to set for 30 minutes. Keep for 2 days in an airtight container.

Fondant Fancies

150 g/5 oz self-raising flour
150 g/5 oz caster sugar
50 g/2 oz ground almonds
150 g/5 oz butter, softened
3 medium eggs, beaten
4 tbsp milk

To decorate:
450 g/1 lb fondant icing sugar
paste food colourings
selection fancy cake
   decorations

Preheat the oven to 180°C/350°F/Gas Mark 4. Line two 12-hole bun trays with 16–18 paper cases, depending on the depth of the tray holes.

Sift the flour into a bowl and stir in the caster sugar and almonds. Add the butter, eggs and milk and beat until smooth.

Spoon into the paper cases and bake for 15–20 minutes until golden and firm to the touch. Turn out to cool on a wire rack. When cool, trim the tops flat if they have peaked slightly.

To decorate the cupcakes, make the fondant icing to a thick coating consistency, following the packet instructions. Divide into batches and colour each separately with a little paste food colouring. Keep each bowl covered with a damp cloth until needed. Spoon some icing over each cupcake, being sure to flood it right to the edge of each cupcake. Top each with a fancy decoration and leave to set for 30 minutes. Keep for 2 days in a cool place.

Lemon & Cardamom Cupcakes with Mascarpone Topping

MAKES 12

1 tsp cardamom seeds
200 g/7 oz butter
50 g/2 oz plain flour
200 g/7 oz self-raising flour
1 tsp baking powder

200 g/7 oz caster sugar
zest of 1 lemon, finely grated
3 medium eggs
100 ml/3½ fl oz natural yogurt
4 tbsp lemon curd

To decorate:
250 g/9 oz tub mascarpone
6 tbsp icing sugar
1 tsp lemon juice
lemon zest strips

Preheat the oven to 180°C/350°F/Gas Mark 4. Line a 12-hole muffin tray with deep paper cases. Crush the cardamom seeds and remove the outer cases. Melt the butter and leave aside to cool.

Sift the flours and baking powder into a bowl and stir in the crushed seeds, sugar and lemon zest. In another bowl, whisk together the eggs and yogurt. Pour into the dry ingredients with the cooled melted butter and beat until combined.

Divide half the mixture between the paper cases, put a teaspoon of lemon curd into each, then top with the remaining mixture. Bake for about 25 minutes until golden.

To make the topping, beat the mascarpone with the icing sugar and lemon juice. Swirl onto each cupcake and top with lemon strips. Eat fresh on day of baking once decorated or store, undecorated, in an airtight container for up to 2 days and add the topping just before serving.

Almond & Cherry Cupcakes
with Rosewater Icing

MAKES 12

50 g/2 oz glacé cherries, plus
   extra for decoration
125 g/4 oz self-raising flour,
   plus extra for dusting

125 g/4 oz soft margarine
125 g/4 oz caster sugar
2 medium eggs
½ tsp almond extract

To decorate:
125 g/4 oz icing sugar
1 tsp lemon juice
pink food colouring

Preheat the oven to 190°C/375°F/Gas Mark 5. Line a 12-hole bun tray with small paper cases. Wash the glacé cherries, then dry them thoroughly. Chop the cherries, then dust lightly in flour and set aside.

Sift the flour into a bowl, then add the margarine, sugar, eggs and extract. Beat until smooth for about 2 minutes, then fold in the chopped cherries.

Spoon into the paper cases. Bake for 15–20 minutes until golden and springy in the centre. Turn out to cool on a wire rack.

To decorate, mix the icing sugar with the lemon juice and 2 tsp water to form a smooth glacé icing. Add a little pink food colouring and drizzle over the top of each cupcake. Place a halved cherry on top and leave to set for 30 minutes. Keep for 2–3 days in an airtight container.

Pink Butterfly Cakes

MAKES 12

150 g/5 oz butter,
softened at room
temperature
150 g/5 oz caster sugar
3 medium eggs, beaten
1 tsp vanilla extract

150 g /5 oz self-raising flour
½ tsp baking powder

To decorate:
pink and brown paste
food colouring

225 g/8 oz ready-to-roll
sugarpaste icing
1 batch cream cheese
frosting (*see* page 67)
tubes of gel writing icing

Preheat the oven to 180°C/350°F/Gas Mark 4 and line a 12-hole muffin tray with deep paper cases.

Place the butter, sugar, eggs and vanilla extract in a bowl and then sift in the flour and baking powder. Beat together for about 2 minutes with an electric hand mixer until pale and fluffy. Spoon into the paper cases and bake for 20–25 minutes until firm and golden. Cool on a wire rack.

To decorate the cupcakes, colour 200 g/7 oz of the sugarpaste pale pink and colour the remainder brown. Roll out the sugarpaste thinly and, using a cutter or the template on page 349, cut out 4 petal shapes for the wings for each cupcake and set them on nonstick baking parchment or clingfilm. Cut out 48 shapes altogether and leave to dry flat until firm (about 2 hours). Colour the cream cheese icing bright pink and place in a piping bag fitted with a star nozzle.

Pipe a swirl of pink icing to cover the top of each cupcake and then press 4 wings on top of each. Mould the brown icing into a thin body shape and place on each cupcake. Pipe dots on the wings with tubes of gel writing icing. Keep for 2 days in an airtight container in a cool place.

Chocolate Delights

Chocolate Mud Cupcakes

MAKES 16

50 g/5 oz butter, softened
150 g/5 oz golden caster sugar
3 medium eggs, beaten
125 g/4 oz self-raising flour
25 g/1 oz cocoa powder

To decorate:
75 g/3 oz milk chocolate
75 g/3 oz unsalted butter,
  softened
150 g/5 oz golden icing

sugar, sifted
white and dark chocolate
  sprinkles

Preheat the oven to 190°C/375°F/Gas Mark 5. Line one or two bun trays with 16 foil or paper cases.

Place the butter, caster sugar and eggs in a large bowl and then sift in the flour and cocoa powder. Whisk together until smooth for about 2 minutes, then spoon into the cases, filling them two-thirds full.

Bake for about 14 minutes until well risen and springy to the touch. Cool on a wire rack.

To make the frosting, break the chocolate into squares and melt in a heatproof bowl over a pan of barely simmering water. Set aside to cool. Beat the butter and sugar together until fluffy, then whisk in the cooled melted chocolate. Swirl over the cupcakes with a flat-bladed knife. Scatter over the sprinkles. Keep for 3 days in a cool place.

White Chocolate Cupcakes

MAKES 12

200 g/7 oz butter
125 g/4 oz white chocolate
50 g/2 oz plain flour
200 g/7 oz self-raising flour

1 tsp baking powder
200 g/7 oz caster sugar
finely grated zest of ½ lemon
3 medium eggs

100 ml/3½ fl oz natural yogurt
250 g/9 oz white chocolate,
   chopped, to decorate

Preheat the oven to 180°C/350°F/Gas Mark 4. Line a 12-hole deep muffin tray with paper cases. Melt the butter and leave aside to cool.

Coarsely grate or chop the white chocolate. Sift the flours and baking powder into a bowl and stir in the sugar, lemon zest and chopped white chocolate.

In another bowl, whisk together the eggs and yogurt. Pour into the dry ingredients with the cooled melted butter and beat until combined. Spoon into the paper cases and bake for about 25 minutes until firm and golden.

To decorate the cupcakes, melt one quarter of the white chocolate in a heatproof bowl standing over a pan of barely simmering water. Spread the melted chocolate out onto a clean plastic board. When almost set, make into curls by pulling a sharp knife through the chocolate (*see* pages 76 and 134). Refrigerate for 30 minutes to set.

Melt the remaining white chocolate, then spoon over the cupcakes and leave for about 10 minutes until cooled and half set. Top each cupcake while still wet with the white chocolate curls and leave to set for 30 minutes. Keep for 2 days in the refrigerator.

Double Chocolate Chip Cupcakes

MAKES 14

125 g/4 oz soft margarine
125g/4 oz golden caster sugar
2 medium eggs, beaten
25 g/1 oz cocoa powder

175 g/6 oz self-raising flour
1 tsp baking powder
50 g/2 oz milk
    chocolate chips

50 g/2 oz dark or white
    chocolate chips
1 tbsp milk

Preheat the oven to 180°C/350°F/Gas Mark 4. Line one or two bun trays with
14 small paper cases.

Place the margarine and sugar in a large bowl with the eggs and sift in the cocoa powder,
flour and baking powder. Beat for about 2 minutes until smooth, then fold in the chocolate
chips with the milk.

Spoon into the paper cases and bake for 15–20 minutes until firm. Place on a wire rack
to cool. Keep for 4–5 days in an airtight container

Chocolate Fudge Flake Cupcakes

MAKES 12 LARGE CUPCAKES OR 18 FAIRY CAKES

125 g/4 oz self-raising flour
25 g/1 oz cocoa powder
125 g/4 oz soft margarine
125 g/4 oz soft light
    brown sugar

2 medium eggs, beaten
2 tbsp milk

To decorate:
25 g/1 oz butter

50 g/2 oz golden syrup
15 g/½ oz cocoa powder
125 g/4 oz golden icing sugar
25 g/1 oz cream cheese
40 g/1½ oz chocolate flake bars

Preheat the oven to 180°C/350°F/Gas Mark 4. Line a 12-hole muffin tray with deep paper cases, or one or two bun trays with 18 fairy-cake cases.

Sift the flour and cocoa powder into a large bowl, add the margarine, sugar, eggs and milk and whisk with an electric beater for about 2 minutes until smooth.

Divide the mixture between the paper cases and bake for about 20 minutes for the larger cupcakes and 15 minutes for the fairy cakes until a skewer inserted into the middle comes out clean. Turn out to cool on a wire rack.

To make the topping, melt the butter with the syrup and cocoa powder in a pan. Cool, then whisk in the icing sugar until the mixture has thickened, and beat in the cream cheese. Spread the frosting over the cupcakes. Chop the flake bar into small chunks, then place one chunk in the centre of each cupcake. Keep for 2–3 days in the refrigerator.

**MAKES 12 LARGE
CUPCAKES OR 24
SMALL CUPCAKES**

Black Forest Cupcakes

1 tbsp cocoa powder
2 tbsp boiling water
175 g/6 oz self-raising flour
1 tsp baking powder
125 g/4 oz soft tub margarine
175 g/6 oz soft dark
    brown sugar

2 medium eggs
3 tbsp milk

To decorate:
125 g/4 oz dark chocolate
4 tbsp seedless raspberry
    jam, warmed

150 ml/¼ pint double cream
1 tbsp kirsch (optional)
12 natural-coloured
    glacé cherries

Preheat the oven to 180°C/350°F/Gas Mark 4. Line a 12-hole muffin tray with large paper cases, or one or two bun trays with 24 small paper cases. Blend the cocoa powder with the boiling water and leave to cool.

Sift the flour and baking powder into a bowl and add the margarine, sugar, eggs, milk and the cocoa mixture. Whisk together for about 2 minutes until smooth, then spoon into the paper cases.

Bake for 15–20 minutes until springy to the touch. Cool in the tins for 5 minutes, then turn out onto a wire rack to cool.

To decorate the cupcakes, melt the chocolate and spread it out to cool on a clean plastic board. When it is almost set, pull a sharp knife through the chocolate to make curls. Refrigerate these until needed. Brush the top of each cupcake with a little raspberry jam. Whisk the cream until it forms soft peaks, then fold in the kirsch, if using. Pipe or swirl the cream on top of each cupcake. Top with chocolate curls and whole glacé cherries for the large muffins or halved cherries for the smaller ones. Eat fresh or keep for 1 day in the refrigerator.

Mocha Cupcakes

MAKES 12

125 g/4 oz soft margarine
125 g/4 oz golden caster sugar
150 g/5 oz self-raising flour
2 tbsp cocoa powder
2 medium eggs

1 tbsp golden syrup
2 tbsp milk

To decorate:
225 g/8 oz golden icing sugar

125 g/4 oz unsalted
  butter, softened
2 tsp coffee extract
12 cape gooseberries, papery
  covering pulled back

Preheat the oven to 180°C/350°F/Gas Mark 4. Line a 12-hole muffin tray with deep paper cases.

Place the margarine and sugar in a large bowl, then sift in the flour and cocoa powder. In another bowl, beat the eggs with the syrup, then add to the cocoa mixture. Whisk everything together with the milk using an electric beater for 2 minutes, or by hand with a wooden spoon.

Divide the mixture between the cases, filling them three-quarters full. Bake for about 20 minutes until the centres are springy to the touch. Turn out to cool on a wire rack.

Make the frosting by sifting the icing sugar into a bowl. Add the butter, coffee extract and 1 tbsp hot water. Beat until fluffy, then swirl onto each cupcake with a flat-bladed knife. Top each with a fresh cape goosberry. Keep for 2 days in a cool place.

Chocolate & Cranberry Cupcakes

MAKES 12

125 g/4 oz soft margarine
125 g/4 oz golden
   caster sugar
2 medium eggs
175 g/6 oz self-raising flour
25 g/1 oz cocoa powder

1 tsp baking powder
2 tbsp milk
125 g/4 oz milk
   chocolate chips
50 g/2 oz dried cranberries

To decorate:
25 g/1 oz cocoa powder
40 g/1 ½ oz unsalted butter
125 g/4 oz golden icing sugar
25g/1 oz dried cranberries

Preheat the oven to 180°C/350°F/Gas Mark 4. Line a muffin tray with 12 deep paper cases.

Place the margarine, sugar and eggs in a bowl, then sift in the flour, cocoa powder and baking powder. Add the milk and beat until smooth. Then fold in the chocolate chips and cranberries.

Spoon into the paper cases and bake for 15–20 minutes until firm in the centre.
Remove to a wire rack to cool.

To decorate the cupcakes, blend the cocoa powder with 1 tbsp hot water until smooth. Cool for 5 minutes. Beat the butter and icing sugar together and then beat in the cocoa mixture. Place in a piping bag with a plain nozzle and pipe swirls on top of each cupcake. Top with dried cranberries. Keep for 2–3 days in the refrigerator.

Rocky Road Cupcakes

MAKES 14–18

125 g/4 oz self-raising flour
25 g/1 oz cocoa powder
125 g/4 oz soft dark
brown sugar
125 g/4 oz soft margarine

2 medium eggs, beaten
2 tbsp milk

To decorate:
75 g/3 oz dark chocolate,

broken into squares
40 g/1½ oz butter
75 g/3 oz mini marshmallows
40 g/1½ oz chopped
mixed nuts

Preheat the oven to 180°C/350°F/Gas Mark 4. Line bun trays with 14–18 paper cases or silicone cupcake moulds, depending on the depth of the holes.

Sift the flour and cocoa powder into a large bowl. Add the sugar, margarine, eggs and milk and whisk with an electric beater for about 2 minutes until smooth.

Divide the mixture evenly between the paper cases and bake for about 20 minutes until a skewer inserted into the middle comes out clean. Remove the tray from the oven but leave the oven on.

To make the topping, gently melt the chocolate and butter together in a small pan over a low heat. Place the melted chocolate mixture in an icing bag made of greaseproof paper and snip away the end. Pipe a little of the mixture on top of each cupcake, then scatter the marshmallows and nuts over each one and return to the oven. Bake for 2–3 minutes to soften the marshmallows. Remove from the oven and pipe the remaining chocolate over the marshmallows. Leave to cool in the tins for 5 minutes, then remove to cool on a wire rack. Serve warm or cold. Keep for 2 days in an airtight container.

Chocolate & Orange Marbled Muffins

MAKES 10–12

175 g/6 oz soft margarine
175 g/6 oz caster sugar
3 medium eggs

175 g/6 oz self-raising flour
1 tsp baking powder
1 tbsp cocoa powder

finely grated zest and juice of
½ orange
4 tbsp clear honey, to glaze

Preheat the oven to 180°C/350°F/Gas Mark 4. Grease two deep 6-hole muffin trays, or line with 10–12 deep paper cases, depending on the depth of the holes.

Put the margarine, sugar, eggs, flour and baking powder into a large mixing bowl. Whisk the mixture together for about 2 minutes until smooth.

Place half the mixture into another bowl and sift over the cocoa, then stir in until blended. Stir the orange juice and zest into the other mixture.

Spoon the cocoa mixture evenly between the prepared tins. Spoon over the orange mixture and, using a flat-bladed knife, swirl through the two mixtures to make a marbled pattern.

Bake for 15–20 minutes until well risen and firm to the touch. Cool in the tins for 5 minutes, then turn out to cool on a wire rack. While still warm, drizzle each muffin with a little clear honey. Keep for 4 days in an airtight container.

Mint Choc Chip Cupcakes

MAKES 12

125 g/4 oz soft margarine
125 g/4 oz golden
caster sugar
2 medium eggs
175 g/6 oz self-raising flour
25 g/1 oz cocoa powder

1 tsp baking powder
75 g/3 oz dark
chocolate chips
25 g/1 oz clear hard
peppermint sweets,
crushed into crumbs

To decorate:
50 g/2 oz unsalted butter
175 g/6 oz icing sugar
peppermint flavouring
or extract
green food colouring
50 g/2 oz chocolate squares

Preheat the oven to 180°C/350°F/Gas Mark 4. Line a 12-hole muffin tray with deep paper cases.

Place the margarine, sugar and eggs in a bowl, then sift in the flour, cocoa powder and baking powder. Beat by hand or with an electric mixer until smooth. Then fold in the chocolate chips and the crushed mints.

Spoon the mixture into the paper cases and bake for 15–20 minutes until firm in the centre. Remove to a wire rack to cool.

Beat the butter and icing sugar together with 1 tbsp warm water, the peppermint extract and the food colouring. Place in a piping bag with a star nozzle and pipe swirls on top of each cupcake. Cut the chocolate into triangles and place one on top of each cake. Keep for 3–4 days in an airtight container in a cool place.

Chocolate & Toffee Cupcakes

MAKES 12–14

125 g/4 oz soft fudge
125 g/4 oz soft margarine
125 g/4 oz golden
    caster sugar

150 g/5 oz self-raising flour
2 tbsp cocoa powder
2 medium eggs
1 tbsp golden syrup

1 batch cream cheese
    frosting (*see* page 67),
    to decorate

Preheat the oven to 180°C/350°F/Gas Mark 4. Line one or two bun trays with 12–14 paper cases, depending on the depth of the holes. Cut one quarter of the fudge into slices for decoration. Chop the rest into small cubes. Set all the fudge aside.

Place the margarine and the sugar in a large bowl and then sift in the flour and cocoa powder. In another bowl, beat the eggs with the syrup, then add to the flour mixture. Whisk together with an electric beater for 2 minutes, or by hand with a wooden spoon until smooth. Gently fold in the fudge cubes.

Spoon the mixture into the cases, filling them three-quarters full. Bake for about 15 minutes until a skewer inserted into the centre comes out clean. Turn out to cool on a wire rack.

Swirl the cream cheese frosting over each cupcake, then finish by topping with a fudge slice. Keep for 3–4 days chilled in a sealed container.

Chocolate, Banana & Pecan Muffins

MAKES 12–14

125 g/4 oz butter, softened
225 g/8 oz soft light
brown sugar
250 g/9 oz ripe bananas,
peeled and mashed
2 medium eggs
1 tsp vanilla extract
½ tsp ground cinnamon

225 g/8 oz plain flour
25 g/1 oz cocoa
powder, sifted
1 tsp baking powder
1 tsp bicarbonate of soda
85 ml/3 fl oz buttermilk
50 g/2 oz pecan nuts, chopped

To decorate:
150 g/5 oz granulated sugar
4 tbsp double cream
50 g/2 oz pecan nuts,
chopped
225 g/8 oz cream cheese
125 g/4 oz golden icing sugar

Preheat the oven to 180°C/350°F/Gas Mark 4. Grease or line one or two deep 12-hole muffin trays with 12–14 deep paper cases, depending on the depth of the holes.

Whisk the butter and sugar together. Add the mashed bananas to the bowl with the eggs and vanilla extract. Sift in the cinnamon, flour, cocoa powder, baking powder and bicarbonate of soda. Add the buttermilk and fold in with the chopped nuts.

Spoon the mixture into the cases. Bake for 25 minutes until well risen and firm in the centre. Cool on a wire rack.

To decorate the muffins, put the granulated sugar in a small pan with 5 tbsp cold water. Heat gently until every grain of sugar has dissolved, then simmer until the mixture turns golden. Holding the pan away from you, as the mixture may spit, add the cream and 1 tbsp water and then stir in the nuts. Remove the pan from the heat to cool slightly. In a bowl, beat the cream cheese with the icing sugar and swirl on top of the muffins. Drizzle with the warm caramel nut sauce and leave to set. Keep for 2–3 days chilled, in a sealed container.

Cappuccino Muffins

MAKES 12–14

125 g/4 oz soft margarine
125 g/4 oz golden
  caster sugar
150 g/5 oz self-raising flour
2 tbsp cocoa powder

2 medium eggs
1 tbsp golden syrup
50 g/2 oz finely grated
  chocolate

To decorate:
150 ml/ ¼ pint double cream
chocolate sprinkles

Preheat the oven to 180°C/350°F/Gas Mark 4. Line one or two bun trays with 12–14 paper cases or silicone moulds, depending on the depth of the holes.

Place the margarine and the sugar in a large bowl, then sift in the flour and cocoa powder. In another bowl, beat the eggs with the syrup, then add to the flour mixture. Whisk together with an electric beater for 2 minutes, or by hand with a wooden spoon, until smooth and then fold in the grated chocolate.

Divide the mixture between the cases, filling them three-quarters full. Bake for about 20 minutes until springy to the touch in the centre. Turn out to cool on a wire rack.

For the decoration, whisk the cream until it forms soft peaks, then swirl over the tops of the muffins with a small palette knife. Scatter the tops with chocolate sprinkles to serve. Eat on the day of decorating or keep for 1 day in a sealed container in the refrigerator.

Mini Chocolate Ripple Muffins

MAKES 24

175 g/6 oz soft margarine
175 g/6 oz caster sugar
3 medium eggs

175 g/6 oz self-raising flour
1 tsp baking powder
1 tbsp cocoa powder

1 tbsp milk
½ tsp vanilla extract

Preheat the oven to 180°C/350°F/Gas Mark 4. Grease a 24-hole mini-muffin tray, or line with paper cases.

Put the margarine, sugar, eggs, flour and baking powder into a large mixing bowl. Whisk for about 2 minutes until smooth, then pour half the mixture into a separate bowl and sift the cocoa powder over it. Stir in the milk until blended. Stir the vanilla extract into the first mixture.

Spoon the cocoa mixture evenly between the prepared tins, then spoon over the vanilla mixture. Using a small spoon, swirl through the two mixtures to make a marbled pattern.

Bake for 12–15 minutes until well risen and firm to the touch. Cool in the tins for 5 minutes, then turn out to cool on a wire rack. Keep in an airtight container for 3–4 days.

Chunky Chocolate Muffins

MAKES 12–14

To decorate:
75 g/3 oz granulated sugar
5 tbsp evaporated milk
125 g/4 oz dark
    chocolate, chopped
40 g/1½ oz unsalted butter

To make the muffins:
125 g/4 oz soft margarine
125 g/4 oz golden
    caster sugar
2 medium eggs, beaten
25 g/1 oz cocoa powder
175 g/6 oz self-raising flour

1 tsp baking powder
2 tbsp milk
50 g/2 oz milk chocolate,
    chopped
50 g/2 oz dark or white
    chocolate, chopped

Make the frosting first in order to allow it to cool. Place the sugar and evaporated milk in a heavy-based pan and stir over a low heat until every grain of sugar has dissolved. Simmer for 5 minutes but do not allow the mixture to boil. Remove from the heat, cool for 5 minutes, and then add the chocolate and butter. Stir until these melt. Pour the mixture into a bowl and chill for 2 hours until thickened.

Preheat the oven to 180°C/350°F/Gas Mark 4. Line one or two deep muffin trays with 12–14 paper cases, depending on the depth of the holes. Place the margarine and sugar in a bowl with the eggs and sift in the cocoa powder, flour and baking powder. Beat with the milk for about 2 minutes until smooth, then fold in the chopped chocolate.

Spoon into the paper cases and bake for 15–20 minutes until firm. Place on a wire rack to cool.

Remove the frosting from the fridge and beat to soften it slightly. Swirl it over the muffins. Keep in a cool place in a sealed container for 3–4 days.

Chocolate Muffins with Irish Cream Topping

MAKES 12–14

125 g/4 oz soft margarine
125 g/4 oz golden
  caster sugar
150 g/5 oz self-raising flour

2 tbsp cocoa powder
2 medium eggs
1 tbsp golden syrup

To decorate:
150 ml/¼ pint double cream
2 tbsp Irish cream liqueur
chocolate sprinkles

Preheat the oven to 180°C/350°F/Gas Mark 4. Line one or two muffin trays with 12–14 deep paper cases, depending on the depth of the holes.

Place the margarine and the sugar in a large bowl, then sift in the flour and cocoa powder. In another bowl, beat the eggs with the syrup and then add to the first bowl. Whisk together with an electric beater for 2 minutes, or by hand with a wooden spoon until smooth.

Divide the mixture between the cases, filling them three-quarters full. Bake for about 20 minutes until the centre is springy to the touch. Turn out to cool on a wire rack.

For the decoration, whip the cream until it forms soft peaks. Gently fold in the cream liqueur, then place the mixture in a piping bag fitted with a plain nozzle. Pipe the cream in swirls, then top with chocolate sprinkles. Keep refrigerated in a sealed container until needed and eat within 2 days.

Very Rich Chocolate Cupcakes

MAKES 12–14

75 g/3 oz self-raising flour
25 g/1 oz cocoa powder
75 g/3 oz soft dark
    brown sugar
75 g/3 oz butter, softened

3 medium eggs
2 tbsp milk

To decorate:
200 g/7 oz dark chocolate

100 ml/3½ fl oz
    whipping cream
1 tbsp liquid glucose
selection chocolate
    decorations

Preheat the oven to 190°C/350°F/Gas Mark 5. Line one or two 12-hole bun trays with 12–14 paper cases, depending on the depth of the holes.

Sift the flour and cocoa powder into a bowl and add the sugar, butter, eggs and milk. Whisk until smooth, then spoon into the paper cases.

Bake for about 14 minutes until just firm to the touch in the centre. Transfer to a wire rack to cool.

To decorate the cupcakes, break the chocolate into pieces and melt in a heatproof bowl standing over a pan of warm water. In another pan, bring the cream to just below boiling, then remove from the heat and stir in the liquid glucose. Add the melted chocolate and stir until smooth and glossy. Spoon over the cupcakes and immediately top each with a chocolate decoration. Leave to set for 30 minutes. Keep for 3 days in an airtight container in a cool place.

Triple Chocolate Muffins

MAKES 9

50 g/2 oz dark chocolate
1 tbsp milk
75 g/3 oz butter or block
   margarine
50 g/2 oz milk chocolate

50 g/2 oz white chocolate
200 g/7 oz self-raising flour
½ tsp bicarbonate of soda
125 g/4 oz soft light
   brown sugar

1 medium egg
150 ml/¼ pint natural yogurt

Preheat the oven to 180°C/350°F/Gas Mark 4. Line nine holes of a 12-hole muffin tray with deep paper cases.

Chop the dark chocolate into rough chunks and place in a small heavy-based pan with the milk and butter. Heat gently until the mixture melts together, then leave to cool.

Chop the milk and white chocolate coarsely and place in a mixing bowl. Sift in the flour and bicarbonate of soda, then stir in the soft light brown sugar.

In another bowl, beat the egg with the yogurt, then add to the dry ingredients in the bowl with the cooled melted mixture and quickly mix together with a fork. Spoon into the cases and bake for about 25 minutes until risen and firm to the touch. Leave in the tray for 2 minutes to firm up and then turn out onto a wire rack to cool. Keep for 5 days in an airtight container.

Orange Drizzle Cupcakes

MAKES 10

75 g/3 oz dark
 chocolate, chopped
125 g/4 oz butter
125 g/4 oz caster sugar
2 medium eggs, beaten

200 g/7 oz self-raising flour
zest of ½ orange,
 finely grated
5 tbsp thick natural yogurt

To decorate:
1 batch orange-flavoured
 buttercream (*see* page 68)
2 tbsp marmalade

Preheat the oven to 190°C/375°F/Gas Mark 5. Grease 10 deep muffin moulds or line
a 12-hole muffin tray with 10 deep paper cases.

Melt the chocolate in a heatproof bowl over a pan of warm water or in the microwave oven
on low for 30 seconds and leave to cool.

Put the butter and sugar in a large bowl and whisk until light and fluffy. Gradually beat in the
eggs, adding a teaspoon of flour with each addition. Beat in the cooled melted chocolate, then
sift in the flour. Add the orange zest and yogurt to the bowl and whisk until smooth.

Spoon the mixture into the paper cases and bake for about 25 minutes until well risen and
springy to the touch. Leave for 2 minutes in the moulds or tray, then turn out onto a wire rack.

To decorate, fill a piping bag fitted with a star nozzle with the buttercream and pipe swirls
on top of each cupcake. Warm the marmalade and place small drizzles around the sides of
the cupcakes with a teaspoon. Keep in an airtight container in a cool place for 4 days.

Blondie Cupcakes

**MAKES 14 LARGE OR
24 MINI CUPCAKES**

175 g/6 oz unsalted
   butter, softened
300 g/11 oz caster sugar
3 medium eggs, beaten
1 tsp vanilla extract
200 g/7 oz plain flour

1 tsp baking powder
100 g/3½ oz white
   chocolate chips
90 g/3¼ oz pecan nuts,
   roughly chopped

90 g/3¼ oz ready-to-eat dried
   apricots, roughly chopped
1 tbsp milk
50 g/2 oz white chocolate,
   melted, to decorate

Preheat the oven to 180°C/350°F/Gas Mark 4. Line two muffin trays with 14 deep paper cases, or one mini-muffin tray with 24 paper cases.

Beat the butter with the sugar until light and fluffy, then add the eggs and vanilla extract gradually, beating between each addition. Sift the flour and baking powder into the bowl, then fold the white chocolate chips, nuts and apricots into the mixture along with the milk until evenly combined.

Spoon the mixture into the prepared tins. Bake for about 25 minutes until just firm. Leave in the tray(s) for 10 minutes, then turn out to cool on a wire rack.

Fill a small greaseproof paper icing bag with the melted chocolate and snip away the end. Pipe a drizzle pattern on top of the cupcakes and leave to set for 30 minutes. Keep in an airtight container for 5 days.

Unbaked Chocolate Cupcakes

MAKES 8

For the cases:
450 g/1 lb dark chocolate

For the filling:
50 g/2 oz trifle sponges
2 tbsp sweet sherry or
    orange liqueur

350 g/12 oz strawberries
450 ml/¾ pint double cream

Wash eight ridged deep silicone moulds and dry them with kitchen paper to ensure they are completely free of moisture. Break the chocolate into small pieces and place in a bowl. Set the bowl over a saucepan of warm water and heat the water to barely simmering to melt the chocolate, or place the bowl in the microwave and melt on low in bursts of 30 seconds.

When the chocolate has melted, brush it round the insides of the moulds with a teaspoon or pastry brush, making sure to go into all the ridges. Chill the moulds for 1 hour.

When the chocolate has set, brush on another thicker layer inside the cases and chill again. Once the cases are solid, carefully peel the silicone mould away from the outsides.

Cut a cube of trifle sponge to fit inside a chocolate case, put inside the case and sprinkle the sponge with sherry or liqueur. Place a small or halved strawberry on top of this. Repeat with the remaining chocolate cases. Whip the cream until it forms soft peaks and place in a piping bag fitted with a large star nozzle. Pipe swirls into each case and top with another small or halved strawberry. Refrigerate until needed for up to 24 hours.

For Parties
& Special Occasions

Banoffee Cupcakes

MAKES 10–12

175 g/6 oz soft ripe bananas
125 g/4 oz soft margarine
75 g/3 oz golden caster sugar
1 tbsp milk

2 medium eggs
225 g/8 oz plain flour
1 tbsp baking powder
75 g/3 oz mini soft
    fudge pieces

To decorate:
125 g/ 4oz golden icing sugar
10–12 semi-dried
    banana flakes

Preheat the oven to 180°C/350°F/Gas Mark 4. Line a 12-hole muffin tray with 10–12 deep paper cases, depending on the depth of the holes.

Peel and mash the bananas in a large bowl, then and add the margarine, sugar, milk and eggs. Sift in the flour and baking powder and beat together for about 2 minutes until smooth.

Fold in 50 g/2 oz of the fudge pieces and then spoon the mixture into the paper cases. Bake for about 20 minutes until golden and firm. Remove from the baking trays to a wire rack to cool.

For the decoration, blend the icing sugar with 3–4 tsp cold water to make a thin icing. Drizzle over the top of each cupcake and, while the icing is still wet, top with the remaining mini fudge pieces and the banana flakes. Leave to dry out for 30 minutes to set the icing. Keep in an airtight container for 3 days.

Sunflower Cupcakes

MAKES 18

150 g/5 oz butter, softened
150 g/5 oz caster sugar
3 medium eggs, beaten
150 g/5 oz self-raising flour
½ tsp baking powder

zest and 2 tbsp juice from 1
  small orange

To decorate:
1 batch buttercream (*see*

   page 68)
yellow and orange food
  colourings

Preheat the oven to 180°C/350°F/Gas Mark 4 and line two bun trays with 18 paper fairy-cake cases.

Place the butter, sugar and beaten eggs in a bowl, then sift in the flour and baking powder. Finely grate the zest from the orange into the bowl and squeeze out 2 tbsp juice.

Beat together for about 2 minutes, preferably with an electric hand mixer, until pale and fluffy. Spoon the mixture into the paper cases and bake for about 15 minutes until firm and golden. Cool on a wire rack.

To decorate, colour three-quarters of the buttercream bright yellow and the remainder orange. Place in two piping bags fitted with star nozzles. Pipe a border of straight lines round the outer edges to form petals. Pipe more petals to fill in the centres. Pipe a circle of orange dots in the centre of each to finish. Keep for 3 days in a cool place.

Boys' & Girls' Names

MAKES 16–18

175 g/6 oz self-raising flour
175 g/6 oz caster sugar
175 g/6 oz soft margarine
3 medium eggs, beaten
1 tsp vanilla extract

To decorate:
1 batch buttercream
(*see* page 68)

paste food colourings
sprinkles and decorations
gel writing icing tubes

Preheat the oven to 180°C/350°F/Gas Mark 4. Line two 12-hole bun trays with
12–14 paper fairy-cake cases or silicone moulds, depending on the depth of the holes.

Sift the flour into a bowl and stir together with the caster sugar. Add the margarine, eggs and
vanilla extract and beat together for about 2 minutes until smooth.

Spoon into the cases and bake for 15–20 minutes until golden and firm to the touch.
Turn out on a wire rack. When cool, trim the tops flat if they have peaked slightly.

Divide the buttercream into batches and colour pink, green and yellow. Spread the icing over
the cakes. Coat the edges of each fairy cake with brightly coloured sprinkles, then add a name
in the centre of each one with the writing icing. Keep in an airtight container in a cool place
for 2 days.

Pink Party Piggies

MAKES 12

125 g/4 oz caster sugar
125 g/4 oz soft tub margarine
2 medium eggs
1 tbsp milk
125 g/ 4 oz self-raising flour
½ tsp baking powder

To decorate:
1 batch buttercream
 (*see* page 68)
pink liquid food colouring
pink marshmallows
edible gold or silver balls

Preheat the oven to 190°C/375°F/Gas Mark 5. Line a bun tray with 12 small paper cases.

Place all the cupcake ingredients in a large bowl and beat with an electric mixer for about 2 minutes until smooth. Half-fill the paper cases with the mixture.

Bake for about 15 minutes until firm, risen and golden. Set on a wire rack to cool.

To decorate, mix the buttercream with the pink food colouring until it is pale pink. Spread smoothly over the top of each cupcake with a small palette knife. Cut a slice from a pink marshmallow with wetted scissors, then cut this in half to form the ears and press into the buttercream. Place a large halved marshmallow in the centre to form the snout. Add edible gold or silver balls to form eyes. Keep for 2–3 days sealed in an airtight container.

Teddy Bear Cupcakes

MAKES 14–16

125 g/4 oz self-raising flour
125 g/4 oz caster sugar
125 g/4 oz soft margarine
2 medium eggs, beaten
1 tsp vanilla extract

To decorate:
225 g/8 oz ready-to-roll
  sugarpaste
brown paste food colouring

325 g/11½ oz fondant
  icing sugar, plus extra
  for dusting
6 tbsp royal icing sugar

Preheat the oven to 180°C/350°F/Gas Mark 4. Line two 12-hole bun trays with
14–16 paper fairy-cake cases or silicone moulds, depending on the depth of the holes.

Sift the flour into a bowl and stir together with the caster sugar. Add the margarine,
eggs and vanilla extract and beat together for about 2 minutes until smooth.

Spoon into the cases and bake for 15–20 minutes until golden and firm to the touch.
Turn out on a wire rack. When cool, trim the tops flat if they have peaked slightly.

Colour the sugarpaste icing golden brown. Dust a small board with icing sugar. Roll the
coloured sugarpaste thinly and stamp out bear shapes with a small cutter or trace round
the pattern on page 346 and mark on to the sugarpaste with a sharp knife. Leave to dry for
30 minutes.

Mix the fondant icing sugar with enough cold water to form a stiff shiny icing of coating
consistency and colour this light brown. Flood the icing on top of each cupcake and, while
still wet, place the bear shape onto this. Mix the royal icing sugar with a little water to make
a stiff paste and then pipe on eyes, a nose and buttons. Leave to set for 30 minutes.
Keep for 1 day in an airtight container.

Kitty Faces Cupcakes

MAKES 14–16

125 g/4 oz self-raising flour
125 g/4 oz caster sugar
125 g/4 oz soft margarine
2 medium eggs, beaten
1 tsp vanilla extract

To decorate:
1 batch buttercream
  (*see* page 68)
pink paste food colouring

50 g/2 oz desiccated coconut
Liquorice All Sorts sweets
red gel writing icing tube

Preheat the oven to 180°C/350°F/Gas Mark 4. Line two 12-hole bun trays with 12–14 paper fairy-cake cases or silicone moulds, depending on the depth of the holes.

Sift the flour into a bowl and stir together with the caster sugar. Add the margarine, eggs and vanilla extract and beat together for about 2 minutes until smooth.

Spoon into the cases and bake for 15–20 minutes until golden and firm to the touch. Turn out on a wire rack. When cool, trim the tops flat if they have peaked slightly.

Colour the buttercream pink and spread over the top of each fairy cake. Pour the coconut onto a shallow dish. Press the top of each iced cupcake into the coconut. Cut the sweets to form pink ears, eyes, a jelly nose and whiskers and pipe on a red mouth in red gel icing. Keep in an airtight container in a cool place for 2 days.

Pirate Cupcakes

MAKES 14–16

125 g/4 oz self-raising flour
125 g/4 oz caster sugar
125 g/4 oz soft margarine
2 medium eggs, beaten
1 tsp vanilla extract

To decorate:
125 g/4 oz buttercream
   (*see* page 68)
450 g/1 lb ready-to-roll
   sugarpaste

pink, yellow, blue and black
   paste food colouring
small sweets and edible
   coloured balls
small tube red gel icing

Preheat the oven to 180°C/350°F/Gas Mark 4. Line two 12-hole bun trays with 14–16 paper fairy-cake cases or silicone moulds, depending on the depth of the holes.

Sift the flour into a bowl and stir together with the caster sugar. Add the margarine, eggs and vanilla extract and beat together for about 2 minutes until smooth.

Divide the mixture between the cases and bake for 15–20 minutes until golden and firm to the touch. Turn out on a wire rack. When cool, trim the tops flat if they have peaked slightly.

To decorate, lightly coat the top of each cupcake with a little buttercream. Colour the sugarpaste pale pink and roll out thinly on a surface dusted with icing sugar. Stamp out circles 6 cm/2½ inches wide (*see* page 347) and place these on the buttercream to cover the top of each cupcake.

Colour some scraps of sugarpaste blue, some yellow and a small amount black. Make triangular shapes from the blue and yellow icing and place these onto the pink icing at an angle to form hats. Stick coloured edible balls into the icing to decorate the hats. Make thin sausages from the black icing and press these across the cupcakes, then make tiny eye patches from black icing. Stick on a tiny sweet for each eye and pipe on red mouths with the gel icing. Keep for 2 days in an airtight container.

Football Cupcakes

MAKES 12–14

125 g/4 oz self-raising flour
125 g/4 oz caster sugar
125 g/4 oz soft margarine
2 medium eggs, beaten
1 tsp vanilla extract

To decorate:
125 g/4 oz buttercream
  (*see* page 68)
600 g/1 lb 5 oz ready-to-roll
  sugarpaste

black paste
  food colouring

Preheat the oven to 180˚C/350˚F/Gas Mark 4. Line two 12-hole bun trays with
12–14 paper fairy-cake cases or silicone moulds, depending on the depth of the holes.

Sift the flour into a bowl and stir together with the caster sugar. Add the margarine,
eggs and vanilla extract and beat together for about 2 minutes until smooth.

Spoon into the cases and bake for 15–20 minutes until golden and firm to the touch.
Turn out on a wire rack. When cool, trim the tops flat if they have peaked slightly.

To decorate, lightly coat the top of each cupcake with a little buttercream. Roll out the
white sugarpaste on a surface dusted with icing sugar and cut out circles 6 cm/2½ inches
wide (*see* page 347) and place these on the buttercream to cover the top of each cupcake.
Colour 75 g/3 oz of the scraps black.

Using a small icing nozzle as a round guide, stamp out small white and black discs.
Cut six straight edges away from the circles to form hexagons. Dampen the back
of each hexagon with a little water, then stick the black discs between white ones, carefully
matching up all the edges so they fit together. Keep for 3 days in an airtight container.

Birthday Numbers Cupcakes

MAKES 12–14

125 g/4 oz self-raising flour
125 g/4 oz caster sugar
125 g/4 oz soft margarine
2 medium eggs, beaten
1 tsp vanilla extract

To decorate:
225 g/8 oz ready-to-roll
  sugarpaste
paste food colourings

icing sugar, for dusting
1 batch buttercream
  (*see* page 68)
small candles

Preheat the oven to 180°C/350°F/Gas Mark 4. Line one or two 12-hole bun trays with 12–14 paper fairy-cake cases or silicone moulds, depending on the depth of the holes.

Sift the flour into a bowl and stir together with the caster sugar. Add the margarine, eggs and vanilla extract and beat together for about 2 minutes until smooth.

Spoon into the cases and bake for 15–20 minutes until golden and firm to the touch. Turn out on a wire rack. When cool, trim the tops flat if they have peaked slightly.

To decorate, colour batches of sugarpaste in bright colours. Dust a clean surface lightly with icing sugar. Thinly roll each colour of sugarpaste and cut out numbers using a set of cutters or tracing round the patterns on pages 342–43. Leave these for 2 hours to dry and harden.

Using a palette knife, spread the buttercream thickly onto the top of each cupcake. Place a small candle into each cupcake and stand the number up against this. Serve within 8 hours as the numbers may start to soften.

Colourful Letters

125 g/4 oz self-raising flour
125 g/4 oz caster sugar
125 g/4 oz soft margarine
2 medium eggs, beaten
1 tsp vanilla extract

To decorate:
225 g/8 oz ready-to-roll
    sugarpaste
paste food colourings

350 g/12 oz icing
    sugar, sifted, plus extra
    for dusting
small coloured sweets

Preheat the oven to 180°C/350°F/Gas Mark 4. Line two 12-hole bun trays with
12–14 paper fairy-cake cases or silicone moulds, depending on the depth of the holes.

Sift the flour into a bowl and stir together with the caster sugar. Add the margarine,
eggs and vanilla extract and beat together for about 2 minutes until smooth.

Spoon into the cases and bake for 15–20 minutes until golden and firm to the touch.
Turn out on a wire rack. When cool, trim the tops flat if they have peaked slightly.

To decorate, colour batches of sugarpaste in bright colours. Dust a clean surface lightly
with icing sugar. Roll each colour out thinly and cut out letters using a set of cutters
or tracing round the patterns on pages 343–45.

Blend the icing sugar with 1 tsp water to make a glacé icing of coating consistency.
Spread over the top of each cupcake and place a bright letter in the centre of each one.
Decorate round the edges with coloured sweets and leave the cupcakes to dry for
30 minutes. Keep for 3 days in an airtight container.

Fast Cars Cupcakes

MAKES 12–14

125 g/4 oz self-raising flour
1 tbsp cocoa powder
125 g/4 oz caster sugar
125 g/4 oz soft margarine
2 medium eggs, beaten
1 tsp vanilla extract

To decorate:
225 g/8 oz ready-to-roll
    sugarpaste
icing sugar, for dusting
red and blue paste food
    colourings

350 g/12 oz fondant icing
    sugar, sifted
6 tbsp royal icing sugar

Preheat the oven to 180°C/350°F/Gas Mark 4. Line two 12-hole bun trays with 12–14 paper fairy-cake cases or silicone moulds, depending on the depth of the holes.

Sift the flour and cocoa powder into a bowl and stir together with the caster sugar. Add the margarine, eggs and vanilla extract and beat together for about 2 minutes until smooth.

Spoon into the cases and bake for 15–20 minutes until golden and firm to the touch. Turn out on a wire rack. When cool, trim the tops flat if they have peaked slightly.

To decorate, colour half the sugarpaste blue and half red. Dust a clean surface lightly with icing sugar. Roll each colour out thinly and cut out little car shapes, tracing round the pattern on page 349. Leave these for 2 hours to dry and harden.

Blend the fondant icing sugar with enough water to make an icing to a coating consistency. Spread over the top of each cupcake and, while still wet, place a car shape in the centre of each one. Mix the royal icing sugar with enough water to make a piping icing. Place this in a small paper icing bag with the end snipped away. Pipe wheels and windows on the cars and leave the cupcakes to dry for 30 minutes. Keep for 3 days in an airtight container.

Goth Cupcakes

MAKES 12–14

125 g/4 oz self-raising flour
125 g/4 oz caster sugar
125 g/4 oz soft margarine
2 medium eggs, beaten
1 tsp vanilla extract

To decorate:
350 g/12 oz fondant icing
  sugar, sifted
black and green paste
  food colourings

edible silver balls and
  decorations

Preheat the oven to 180°C/350°F/Gas Mark 4. Line two 12-hole bun trays with
12–14 paper fairy-cake cases or silicone moulds, depending on the depth of the holes.

Sift the flour into a bowl and stir together with the caster sugar. Add the margarine,
eggs and vanilla extract and beat together for about 2 minutes until smooth.

Spoon into the cases and bake for 15–20 minutes until golden and firm to the touch.
Turn out on a wire rack. When cool, trim the tops flat if they have peaked slightly.

To decorate, blend the fondant icing sugar with enough water to make a coating consistency.
Colour half the icing black and half green. Spread over the top of each cupcake and place
the silver balls round the outer edges. Decorate with metallic cake shapes and dry for
30 minutes. Keep for 2 days in a cool place in an airtight container.

Jellybean Cupcakes

MAKES 12–14

125 g/4 oz self-raising flour
125 g/4 oz caster sugar
125 g/4 oz soft margarine
2 medium eggs, beaten
1 tsp vanilla extract

To decorate:
1 batch buttercream
   (*see* page 68)
colourful jellybeans or
   candied jelly shapes

Preheat the oven to 180°C/350°F/Gas Mark 4. Line two 12-hole bun trays with 12–14 paper fairy-cake cases or silicone moulds, depending on the depth of the holes.

Sift the flour into a bowl and stir together with the caster sugar. Add the margarine, eggs and vanilla extract and beat together for about 2 minutes until smooth.

Spoon into the cases and bake for 15–20 minutes until golden and firm to the touch. Turn out to cool on a wire rack.

When completely cold, swirl buttercream icing all over the tops of the cupcakes and decorate by pressing on coloured jellybeans. Keep for 3 days in a cool place in an airtight container.

Pink Flower Cupcakes

MAKES 12

150 g/5 oz butter, softened
150 g/5 oz caster sugar
3 medium eggs, beaten
1 tsp vanilla extract
150 g /5 oz self-raising flour
½ tsp baking powder

To decorate:
pink paste food colouring
650 g/1 lb 7 oz ready-to-roll
   sugarpaste
½ batch cream cheese
   frosting (*see* page 67)

Preheat the oven to 180°C/350°F/Gas Mark 4 and line a 12-hole muffin tray with deep paper cases.

Place the butter, sugar, eggs and vanilla extract in a bowl, then sift in the flour and baking powder. Beat together for about 2 minutes with an electric hand mixer until pale and fluffy. Spoon into the paper cases and bake for 20–25 minutes until firm and golden. Cool on a wire rack.

To decorate the cupcakes, first line a 12-hole egg box with foil. Colour 175 g/6 oz of the sugarpaste pink. Roll it out thinly and, using a cutter or the template on page 349, cut out 12 flower shapes. Use a cocktail stick to mark ridges on the petals and mould the icing in your hand to form flower shapes, then leave in the foil-lined egg boxes for 2 hours.

When the flowers are nearly hardened, roll out the remaining white sugarpaste thinly on a surface dusted with icing sugar and cut out circles 6 cm/2½ inches wide (*see* page 347). Spread half the cream cheese frosting thinly over each cake and top with a sugarpaste disc. Top each cupcake with a flower, pressing it gently to fix, and pipe a little frosting into the centre of each flower. Keep in a sealed container in a cool place for up to 2 days.

Prize Rosette Cupcakes

MAKES 12

125 g/4 oz self-raising flour
125 g/4 oz caster sugar
125 g/4 oz soft margarine
2 medium eggs, beaten
1 tsp vanilla extract

To decorate:
125 g/4 oz buttercream
 (*see* page 68)
600 g/1 lb 4 oz ready-to-roll
 sugarpaste

red, yellow and blue paste
 food colourings
gel writing icing tubes

Preheat the oven to 180°C/350°F/Gas Mark 4. Line a 12-hole bun tray with paper cases or silicone moulds.

Sift the flour into a bowl and stir together with the caster sugar. Add the margarine, eggs and vanilla extract and beat together for about 2 minutes until smooth.

Spoon the mixture into the cases and bake for 15–20 minutes until golden and firm to the touch. Turn out on a wire rack. When cool, trim the tops flat if they have formed peaks.

To decorate, spread buttercream over the cupcakes and set aside. Break the sugarpaste into three batches and colour each a different colour. Roll out the sugarpaste on a surface lightly dusted with icing sugar and stamp out a fluted circle 6 cm/2½ inches wide with a pastry cutter. Out of the centre of this circle, cut away a small plain disc 3 cm/1 inch wide and discard. Take a cocktail stick and roll this back and forth in the sugarpaste icing until it begins to frill up. Take the frilled circle and place in the buttercream, fluting up the edges. Make another fluted circle in a contrasting colour and place this inside the first layer. Stamp out a plain circle and place this in the centre. Write prizes, such as '1st', '2nd' and 3rd', in gel icing in the centres. Keep for 3 days in a cool place in an airtight container.

Pink Candle Cupcakes

MAKES 12

75 g/3 oz fresh raspberries
150 g/5 oz butter, softened
150 g/5 oz caster sugar
175 g/6 oz self-raising flour
3 medium eggs
1 tsp vanilla extract

To decorate:
1 batch cream cheese
    frosting (*see* page 67)
pink liquid food colouring
small pink candles

Preheat the oven to 180°C/350°F/Gas Mark 4. Line a 12-hole muffin tray with deep paper cases.

Press the raspberries through the sieve to make a purée. Cream the butter and sugar in a bowl, then sift in the flour. In another bowl, beat the eggs with the vanilla extract, then add to the butter and sugar mixture. Beat until smooth, then fold in the purée. Spoon into the cases, filling them three-quarters full.

Bake for about 18 minutes until firm to the touch in the centre. Turn out to cool on a wire rack.

Colour the frosting pink with a few dots of food colouring. Place in a piping bag fitted with a star nozzle and pipe large swirls on top of each cupcake. Top each cupcake with a tiny candle. Keep for 3 days in an airtight container in a cool place.

Blue Bow Cupcakes

MAKES 12

150 g/5 oz butter, softened
150 g/5 oz caster sugar
175 g/6 oz self-raising flour
3 medium eggs
1 tsp vanilla extract

To decorate:
1 batch cream cheese
    frosting (*see* page 67)
blue paste
    food colouring

narrow blue ribbon
cocktail sticks

Preheat the oven to 180°C/350°F/Gas Mark 4. Line a 12-hole muffin tray with deep paper cases.

Place the butter and sugar in a bowl, then sift in the flour. In another bowl, beat the eggs with the vanilla extract, then add to the bowl. Beat until smooth, then spoon into the cases, filling them three-quarters full.

Bake for about 18 minutes until firm to the touch in the centre. Turn out to cool on a wire rack.

To decorate the cupcakes, colour the frosting with a few dots of blue food colouring. Place in a piping bag fitted with a star nozzle and pipe large swirls on top of each cupcake. Make tiny bows from the narrow ribbon and slide each one onto a cocktail stick. Top each cupcake with a tiny bow, being careful to keep the ribbon out of the icing. Keep for 2 days in an airtight container in a cool place. Remember to remove the cocktail sticks and bows before eating the cupcakes.

Starry Cupcakes

MAKES 12

125 g/4 oz butter, softened
125 g/4 oz caster sugar
125 g/4 oz self-raising flour
2 medium eggs
1 tsp vanilla extract

To decorate:
icing sugar, for dusting
225 g/8 oz ready-to-roll
  sugarpaste
dust or paste food colourings

1 batch cream cheese
  frosting (*see* page 67)
edible silver ball decorations
  (optional)
small candles

Preheat the oven to 180°C/350°F/Gas Mark 4. Line a 12-hole muffin tray with deep paper cases.

Place the butter and sugar in a bowl, then sift in the flour. In another bowl, beat the eggs with the vanilla extract, then add to the flour mixture. Beat until smooth, then spoon into the cases, filling them three-quarters full.

Bake for about 18 minutes until firm to the touch in the centre. Turn out to cool on a wire rack.

To decorate the cupcakes, dust a clean flat surface with icing sugar. Colour the sugarpaste in batches of bright colours, such as blue, yellow and orange. Roll each out thinly and cut out stars with a cutter or follow the pattern on page 347. Leave to dry out for 2 hours until firm. Place the frosting in a piping bag fitted with a star nozzle and pipe large swirls on top of each cupcake. Decorate each cupcake with stars, edible silver balls, if using, and small candles. Keep for 2 days in an airtight container in a cool place.

Polka Dot Cupcakes

MAKES 12

150 g/5 oz butter, softened
150 g/5 oz caster sugar
175 g/6 oz self-raising flour

3 medium eggs
1 tsp vanilla extract
2 tbsp milk

To decorate:
1 batch cream cheese
    frosting (*see* page 67)
125 g/4 oz sugarpaste icing
paste food colourings

Preheat the oven to 180°C/350°F/Gas Mark 4. Line a 12-hole muffin tray with paper cases.

Place the butter and sugar in a bowl, then sift in the flour. In another bowl, beat the eggs with the vanilla extract and milk, then add to the flour mixture and beat until smooth. Spoon into the cases, filling them three-quarters full.

Bake for about 18 minutes until firm to the touch in the centre. Turn out to cool on a wire rack.

To decorate the cupcakes, swirl the top of each cupcake with a little cream cheese icing using a small palette knife. Divide the sugarpaste into batches and colour each one separately with paste food colouring. Dust a clean flat surface with icing sugar. Roll out the coloured icing and stamp out small coloured circles with the flat end of an icing nozzle. Press the dots onto the frosting. Keep for for 3 days in a cool place in an airtight container.

New Home Cupcakes

MAKES 14

125 g/4 oz self-raising flour
125 g/4 oz caster sugar
125 g/4 oz soft margarine
2 medium eggs, beaten
1 tsp vanilla extract

To decorate:
125 g/4 oz buttercream
   (*see* page 68)
450 g/1 lb ready-to-roll
   sugarpaste

red, brown and yellow paste
   food colourings
gel writing icing tubes

Preheat the oven to 180°C/350°F/Gas Mark 4. Line two 12-hole bun trays with 14 paper fairy-cake cases or silicone moulds.

Sift the flour into a bowl and stir together with the caster sugar. Add the margarine, eggs and vanilla extract and beat together for about 2 minutes until smooth.

Spoon into the cases and bake for 15–20 minutes until golden and firm to the touch. Turn out on a wire rack. When cool, trim the tops flat if they have peaked slightly.

To decorate, lightly coat the top of each cupcake with a little buttercream. Dust a clean flat surface with icing sugar. Colour half the sugarpaste a pale lemon yellow and roll it out thinly. Cut out circles 6 cm/2½ inches wide and place these over the buttercream and press to smooth down. Colour half the remaining icing brown and the other half red. Roll out thinly on a dusted surface. Cut out small squares in the brown icing and then measure across and cut out a triangular roof shape in red icing. Press the shapes onto the cupcake and pipe on doors, windows and roof tiles in white piping icing. Keep for 3 days in an airtight container.

Valentine Heart Cupcakes

MAKES 12

150 g/5 oz butter, softened
150 g/5 oz caster sugar
3 medium eggs, beaten
1 tsp vanilla extract
2 tbsp milk

150 g/5 oz self-raising flour
½ tsp baking powder

To decorate:
pink and red paste food colouring

225 g/8 oz ready-to-roll
   sugarpaste
icing sugar, for dusting
1 batch cream cheese frosting
   (*see* page 67)

Preheat the oven to 180°C/350°F/Gas Mark 4 and line a 12-hole muffin tray with deep paper cases.

Place the butter, sugar, eggs, vanilla extract and milk in a bowl, then sift in the flour and baking powder. Beat together for about 2 minutes with an electric hand mixer until pale and fluffy. Spoon into the paper cases and bake for 20–25 minutes until firm and golden. Cool on a wire rack.

To decorate, colour one third of the sugarpaste pink and one third red, leaving the rest white. Dust a clean flat surface with icing sugar. Roll out the sugarpaste thinly and, using a cutter or the template on page 348, cut out pink, red and white heart shapes, then leave to dry flat and harden for 2 hours. Colour the cream cheese icing pale pink and place in a piping bag fitted with a star nozzle.

Pipe a swirl on top of each cupcake and decorate with the hearts. Keep in a cool place for up to 2 days.

Ruffled Cupcakes

MAKES 12

125 g/4 oz self-raising flour
125 g/4 oz caster sugar
125 g/4 oz soft margarine

2 medium eggs, beaten
1 tsp lemon juice
1 tbsp milk

To decorate:
125 g/4 oz buttercream
(*see* page 68)
450 g/1 lb ready-to-roll
sugarpaste

Preheat the oven to 180°C/350°F/Gas Mark 4. Line a 12-hole bun tray with paper cases
or silicone moulds.

Sift the flour into a bowl and stir together with the caster sugar. Add the margarine and
eggs and beat together with the lemon juice and milk for about 2 minutes until smooth.

Spoon into the cases and bake for 15–20 minutes until golden and firm to the touch.
Turn out on a wire rack. When cool, trim the tops flat if they have formed peaks. Spread
buttercream over the flat surfaces.

To decorate the cupcakes, dust a clean flat surface with icing sugar. Roll out the sugarpaste
and stamp out a fluted circle 6 cm/2½ inches wide. Cut a small plain 3 cm/1 inch wide
circle out of the centre and discard. Take a cocktail stick and roll this back and forth in the
sugarpaste circle until it begins to frill up. Take the frilled circle and place on the buttercream,
fluting up the edges. Make another fluted circle and cut a break in the ring, then coil this
round inside the first layer. Roll a pea-sized ball and place this in the centre. Serve dusted
with icing sugar. Keep for 3 days in a cool place in an airtight container.

Mini Valentine Heart Cupcakes

MAKES 24

125 g/4 oz soft margarine
125 g/4 oz caster sugar
2 medium eggs, beaten
1 tsp vanilla extract
1 tbsp milk
125 g/4 oz self-raising flour

To decorate:
 pink and red paste food
  colouring
225 g/8 oz ready-to-roll
  sugarpaste

50 g/2 oz ready-made
 royal icing
1 batch cream cheese
 frosting (*see* page 67)

Preheat the oven to 180°C/350°F/Gas Mark 4 and line a 24-hole mini-muffin tray with mini paper cases.

Place the margarine, sugar, eggs, vanilla extract and milk in a bowl, then sift in the flour. Beat together for about 2 minutes with an electric hand mixer until pale and fluffy.

Spoon into the paper cases and bake for 14–18 minutes until firm and golden. Cool on a wire rack.

To decorate, dust a clean flat surface with icing sugar. Colour one third of the sugarpaste pink and one third red. Leave the rest white. Roll out the sugarpaste thinly and, using a cutter or the small heart template on page 348, cut out pink, red and white heart shapes. Press onto a cocktail stick and then secure with a little royal icing. Leave to dry flat and harden for 2 hours on greaseproof paper. Colour the cream cheese frosting pale pink and place in a piping bag fitted with a star nozzle.

Pipe a swirl on top of each cupcake and decorate each one with a heart. Keep in a cool place for up to 2 days. Remember to remove the cocktail sticks before eating the cupcakes.

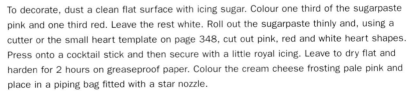

Mother's Day Rose Cupcakes

MAKES 12

125 g/4 oz caster sugar
125 g/4 oz soft
  tub margarine
2 medium eggs
125 g/4 oz self-raising flour

1 tsp baking powder
1 tsp rosewater

To decorate:
50 g/2 oz ready-to-roll

sugarpaste icing
pink paste food colouring
350 g/12 oz fondant
  icing sugar

Preheat the oven to 190°C/375°F/Gas Mark 5. Line a 12-hole bun tray with paper cases.

Place all the cupcake ingredients in a large bowl and beat with an electric mixer for about 2 minutes until smooth. Fill the paper cases halfway up with the mixture. Bake for about 15 minutes until firm, risen and golden. Remove to a wire rack to cool.

To decorate the cupcakes, first line an egg box with foil and set aside. Colour the sugarpaste icing with pink paste food colouring. Make a small cone shape, then roll a pea-sized piece of sugarpaste into a ball. Flatten out the ball into a petal shape and wrap this round the cone shape. Continue adding more petals to make a rose, then trim the thick base, place in the egg box and leave to dry out for 2 hours.

Blend the fondant icing sugar with a little water to make a thick icing of spreading consistency, then colour this pale pink. Smooth over the top of each cupcake and decorate with the roses immediately. Leave to set for 1 hour. Keep for 1 day in an airtight container.

Father's Day Cupcakes

MAKES 14

125 g/4 oz self-raising flour
125 g/4 oz caster sugar
125 g/4 oz soft margarine
2 medium eggs, beaten
1 tsp vanilla extract

To decorate:
1 batch buttercream
  (*see* page 68)
blue, yellow and orange
  paste food colouring

225 g/8 oz ready-to-roll
  sugarpaste
50 g/2 oz royal icing sugar
edible silver balls

Preheat the oven to 180°C/350°F/Gas Mark 4. Line two 12-hole bun trays with 14 paper fairy-cake cases or silicone moulds.

Sift the flour into a bowl and stir together with the caster sugar. Add the margarine, eggs and vanilla extract and beat together for about 2 minutes until smooth.

Spoon into the cases and bake for 15–20 minutes until golden and firm to the touch. Turn out on a wire rack. When cool, trim the tops flat if they have peaked slightly.

To decorate, colour half the buttercream yellow and the other half orange and swirl over the top of each cupcake. Dust a clean flat surface with icing sugar. Colour the sugarpaste light blue and roll out thinly. Stamp out large stars 4 cm/1½ inches wide (*see* pattern page 347) and place these on the buttercream.

Make up the royal icing mix and place in a paper piping bag with the end snipped away and pipe 'Dad' or names on the stars. Decorate with the edible silver balls. Keep for 3 days in an airtight container.

Pink Baby Bow Cupcakes

MAKES 12

125 g/4 oz self-raising flour
125 g/4 oz caster sugar
125 g/4 oz soft margarine
2 medium eggs, beaten
1 tsp vanilla extract
pink paste food colouring

To decorate:
1 batch buttercream
  (*see* page 68)
  pink paste food colouring
225 g/8 oz ready-to-roll
  sugarpaste

Preheat the oven to 180°C/350°F/Gas Mark 4. Line a 12-hole muffin tray with deep paper cases or silicone moulds.

Sift the flour into a bowl and stir together with the caster sugar. Add the margarine, eggs and vanilla extract and beat together with a little pink paste food colouring to give a delicate pink. Beat for about 2 minutes until smooth.

Spoon into the cases and bake for 20 minutes, or until golden and firm to the touch. Turn out on a wire rack. When cool, trim the tops flat if they have peaked slightly.

To decorate, colour the buttercream pale pink, then colour the sugarpaste pink to match the buttercream. Dust a clean flat surface with icing sugar. Roll out the sugarpaste thinly and cut out long narrow strips 1½ cm/½ inch wide. Roll small squares of nonstick baking parchment into narrow tubes and fold the pink icing over these to form loops. Make 24 loops, two for each cupcake, and leave to dry out and firm up for 2 hours. Cut strips to form the ribbon ends of each bow and keep aside on nonstick baking parchment.

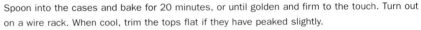

To finish off the cupcakes, spread the top of each one with pink buttercream, carefully remove the loops from the paper and position the bows in the icing. Place the ribbon pieces onto the cupcakes to finish. Keep for 3 days in a cool place in an airtight container.

Winter Wedding Cupcakes

MAKES 12–14

125 g/4 oz butter
125 g/4 oz soft dark
  muscovado sugar
2 medium eggs, beaten
225 g/8 oz self-raising flour
1 tsp ground mixed spice
finely grated zest and 1 tbsp
  juice from 1 orange

1 tbsp black treacle
350 g/12 oz mixed dried fruit

To decorate:
3 tbsp sieved apricot glaze
  (*see* page 72)
450 g/1 lb almond paste
  (*see* page 73)

icing sugar, for dusting
225 g/8 oz ready-to-roll
  sugarpaste
225 g/8 oz royal icing
fancy paper wrappers
  (optional)

Preheat the oven to 180°C/350°F/Gas Mark 4. Line one or two 12-hole muffin trays with 12–14 deep paper cases, depending on the depth of the holes.

Beat the butter and sugar together until light and fluffy, then beat in the eggs a little at a time, adding 1 tsp flour with each addition. Sift in the remaining flour and the spice, add the orange zest and juice, treacle and dried fruit to the bowl and fold together until the mixture is blended. Spoon into the tins and bake for 30 minutes until firm in the centre and a skewer comes out clean. Leave to cool in the tins for 15 minutes, then turn out onto a wire rack. Store undecorated in an airtight container for up to 3 weeks, or freeze until needed.

To decorate the cupcakes, trim the top of each cake level, then brush with apricot glaze. Roll out the almond paste and cut out eight discs 6 cm/2½ inches wide. Place these over the glaze and press level. Leave to dry for 24 hours if possible.

Dust a clean flat surface with icing sugar. Roll out the sugarpaste and stamp out holly leaf and ivy shapes, or use the patterns on pages 348 and 349. Leave to dry for 2 hours on nonstick baking parchment or clingfilm. Swirl the royal icing over the top of each cupcake. Press in the holly and ivy shapes and leave to set for 2 hours. Once decorated, keep in an airtight container for 3 days.

Butterfly Wings
& Flowers Cupcakes

MAKES 12–14

150 g/5 oz butter, softened
150 g/5 oz caster sugar
175 g/5 oz self-raising flour
3 medium eggs, beaten
1 tsp lemon juice
2 tbsp milk

To decorate:
350 g/12 oz ready-to-roll
  sugarpaste
paste food colourings
icing sugar, for dusting
1 batch cream cheese

frosting (*see* page 67)
gel icing tubes

Preheat the oven to 180°C/350°F/Gas Mark 4. Line one or two 12-hole muffin trays with 12–14 deep paper cases, depending on the depth of the holes.

Place the butter and sugar in a bowl, then sift in the flour. Add beaten eggs to the bowl with the lemon juice and milk and beat until smooth. Spoon into the cases, filling them three-quarters full.

Bake for about 18 minutes until firm to the touch in the centre. Turn out to cool on a wire rack.

To decorate, colour the sugarpaste in batches of lilac, blue, pink and yellow. Dust a clean flat surface with icing sugar. Roll out the sugarpaste thinly and mark out daisy shapes (*see* page 234) and butterfly wings following the pattern on page 346. Leave these to dry for 30 minutes until firm enough to handle.

Place the frosting in a piping bag fitted with a star nozzle and pipe swirls onto each cupcake. Press the wings and flowers onto the frosting and pipe on decorations with small gel icing tubes. Keep in an airtight container in a cool place for 3 days.

Quilted Cupcakes

MAKES 12–14

125 g/4 oz self-raising flour
125 g/4 oz caster sugar
125 g/4 oz soft margarine
2 medium eggs, beaten
1 tsp lemon juice

To decorate:
125 g/4 oz buttercream
  (*see* page 68)
450 g/1 lb ready-to-roll
  sugarpaste

edible gold or
  silver balls

Preheat the oven to 180°C/350°F/Gas Mark 4. Line two 12-hole bun trays with 12–14 foil cases, depending on the depth of the holes.

Sift the flour into a bowl and stir together with the caster sugar. Add the margarine and eggs and beat together with the lemon juice for about 2 minutes until smooth.

Spoon into the cases and bake for 15–20 minutes until golden and firm to the touch. Turn out on a wire rack. When cool, trim the tops flat if they have peaked slightly.

To decorate, lightly coat the top of each cupcake with a little buttercream. Dust a clean flat surface with icing sugar. Roll out the sugarpaste and stamp out circles 6 cm/2½ inches wide (*see* page 347). Place these on the buttercream to cover the top of each cupcake. Take a palette knife and press lines into the icing, then mark across in the opposite direction to make small squares. Place an edible gold or silver ball into the corner of each square. Keep for 3 days in an airtight container in a cool place.

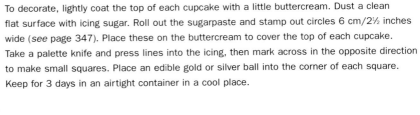

Hearts & Flowers Cupcakes

MAKES 12

150 g/5 oz butter, softened
150 g/5 oz caster sugar
175 g/6 oz self-raising flour
3 medium eggs, beaten

1 tsp lemon juice
1 tbsp milk
To decorate:
350 g/12 oz sugarpaste icing

paste food colourings
icing sugar, for dusting
1 batch cream cheese
frosting (*see* page 67)

Preheat the oven to 180°C/350°F/Gas Mark 4. Line a 12-hole muffin tray with deep paper cases.

Place the butter and sugar in a bowl, then sift in the flour. Add the beaten eggs to the bowl with the lemon juice and milk and beat until smooth. Spoon into the cases, filling them three-quarters full.

Bake for about 18 minutes until firm to the touch in the centre. Turn out to cool on a wire rack.

To decorate, colour the sugarpaste in batches in any colours you like. Dust a clean flat surface with icing sugar. Roll out the sugarpaste thinly and stamp out daisies using a flower stamp (*see also* page 234), then roll out some more sugarpaste thinly and cut out small heart shapes (*see* page 348). Leave these to dry out for 30 minutes until firm enough to handle.

Place the frosting in a piping bag fitted with a star nozzle. Pipe swirls onto each cupcake. Press the flowers and hearts onto the frosting. Keep in an airtight container in a cool place for 3 days.

Silver Wedding Celebration Cupcakes

MAKES 24

150 g/5 oz butter, softened
150 g/5 oz caster sugar
150 g/5 oz self-raising flour
25 g/1 oz ground almonds
3 medium eggs, beaten

1 tsp almond extract
2 tbsp milk

To decorate:
350 g/12 oz sugarpaste icing

edible silver dusting powder
450 g/1 lb fondant icing sugar
24 small silver ribbon bows

Preheat the oven to 180°C/350°F/Gas Mark 4. Line two 12-bun trays with silver foil cases.

Place the butter and sugar in a bowl, then sift in the flour and stir in the almonds.
Add the beaten eggs to the bowl along with the almond extract and milk and beat until
smooth. Spoon into the cases, filling them three-quarters full.

Bake for about 18 minutes until firm to the touch in the centre. Turn out onto a wire rack.
Once cool, trim the tops of the cupcakes if they have peaked.

To decorate the cupcakes, first line an egg box with foil. Roll the sugarpaste into pea-sized balls
and mould each one into a petal shape. Mould a cone shape and wrap a petal completely
round this. Take another petal and wrap round the first, overlapping. Continue wrapping 4–5
petals round until a rose has formed. Pull the thick base away, flute out the petals and place
in the egg box. Repeat until you have 24 roses. Leave them to dry out for 2–4 hours. When
they are firm, brush edible silver dust lightly over each rose with a clean paintbrush.

Make up the fondant icing sugar with water, according to the packet instructions, to a thick
icing of a spreading consistency. Spread over the top of each cupcake. Work quickly, as this
icing will set. Press a rose into the icing and place a thin silver bow on each cupcake. Leave
to set for 30 minutes. Keep in a cool place for 2 days. Remove the bows before eating.

Golden Wedding Celebration Cupcakes

MAKES 24

125 g/4 oz self-raising flour
125 g/4 oz caster sugar
125 g/4 oz soft margarine
2 medium eggs, beaten
1 tsp lemon juice

To decorate:
125 g/4 oz buttercream
(*see* page 68)
icing sugar, for dusting

700 g/1½ lb ready-to-roll
sugarpaste
yellow paste food colouring
thin gold ribbon, curled

Preheat the oven to 180°C/350°F/Gas Mark 4. Line two 12-hole bun trays with small gold foil cases.

Sift the flour into a bowl and stir together with the caster sugar. Add the margarine and eggs and beat together with the lemon juice for about 2 minutes until smooth.

Spoon into the cases and bake for 15–20 minutes until golden and firm to the touch. Turn out on a wire rack. When cool, trim the tops flat if they have peaked slightly.

To decorate, lightly coat the top of each cupcake with a little buttercream. Dust a clean flat surface with icing sugar. Roll out two thirds of the sugarpaste and stamp out circles 6 cm/2½ inches wide (*see* page 347) and place these on the buttercream to cover the top of each cupcake.

Colour one eighth of the sugarpaste a deep yellow and mould this into thin sausage shapes. Leave these to dry for about 2 hours until firm. Roll out the remaining white sugarpaste and mark out small squares 4 x 4 cm (¾ x ¾ inch). Wrap a square round a yellow centre to form a lily and press the ends together. Make up all the lilies and place on the cupcakes. Cut short thin strips of gold paper ribbon and pull along the blade of a pair of scissors to curl and place on the cakes. Keep for 3 days in an airtight container in a cool place. Remove the ribbons before eating.

Christening Day Daisy Cupcakes

MAKES 12

150 g/5 oz butter, softened
150 g/5 oz caster sugar
150 g/5 oz self-raising flour
3 medium eggs, beaten
1 tsp lemon juice
2 tbsp milk

To decorate:
icing sugar, for dusting
125 g/4 oz sugarpaste icing
yellow gel icing tube

1 batch cream cheese
frosting (*see* page 67)
yellow paste food colouring

Preheat the oven to 180˚C/350˚F/Gas Mark 4. Line a 12-hole muffin tray with deep paper cases.

Place the butter and sugar in a bowl, then sift in the flour. Add the beaten eggs to the bowl with the lemon juice and milk and beat until smooth. Spoon into the cases, filling them three-quarters full.

Bake for about 18 minutes until firm to the touch in the centre. Turn out to cool on a wire rack.

To decorate, dust a clean flat surface with icing sugar. Roll out the sugarpaste thinly and stamp out daisy shapes. Leave these to dry out for 30 minutes until firm enough to handle. Pipe a small yellow gel dot into the centre of each one. Colour the frosting pale yellow, then spread onto the cakes using a palette knife. Press the daisies onto the frosting. Keep in an airtight container in a cool place for 3 days.

Rose Petal Cupcakes

MAKES 12

125 g/4 oz self-raising flour
125 g/4 oz butter, softened
125 g/4 oz golden
   caster sugar
2 medium eggs, beaten
1 tbsp rosewater

To decorate:
1 egg white
about 80 small dry
   rose petals
caster sugar, for dusting
175 g/6 oz icing sugar

1 tbsp glycerine
2 tbsp rosewater
pink food colouring

Preheat the oven to 180°C/350°F/Gas Mark 4. Line a 12-hole bun tray with foil cases.

Sift the flour into a bowl and add the butter, sugar, eggs and rosewater. Beat for about 2 minutes until smooth, then spoon into the paper cases.

Bake in the centre of the oven for about 14 minutes until well risen and springy in the centre. Transfer to a wire rack to cool. Keep undecorated for up to 2 days in an airtight container.

To decorate, first place a large piece of nonstick baking parchment on a flat surface. Beat the egg white until frothy, then brush thinly over the rose petals. Set the petals on the paper. Dust with caster sugar and leave for 3 hours until dry and sparkling.

Beat the icing sugar with the glycerine and rosewater and add enough colouring to give a pale pink colour. Spread over the top of each cupcake and add a circle of rose petals, working quickly as the icing will begin to set. Leave for 30 minutes before serving. Eat on the day of decorating.

Red & White Cut–Out Heart Cupcakes

MAKES 24

125 g/4 oz self-raising flour
125 g/4 oz caster sugar
125 g/4 oz soft margarine
2 medium eggs, beaten
1 tsp vanilla extract

To decorate:
125 g/4 oz buttercream
 (*see* page 68)

450 g/1 lb ready-to-roll
 sugarpaste
red paste food colouring

Preheat the oven to 180°C/350°F/Gas Mark 4. Line two 12-hole bun trays with paper or foil cases.

Sift the flour into a bowl and stir together with the caster sugar. Add the margarine and eggs and beat together with the vanilla extract for about 2 minutes until smooth.

Spoon into the cases and bake for 15–20 minutes until golden and firm to the touch. Turn out on a wire rack. When cool, trim the tops flat if they have peaked slightly.

To decorate, lightly coat the top of each cupcake with a little buttercream. Colour half the sugarpaste red. Dust a clean flat surface with icing sugar. Roll out the sugarpaste and stamp out circles 6 cm/2½ inches wide (*see* page 347). Place a small heart cutter centrally or trace round the pattern on page 349 and cut out heart shapes.

Carefully take a white outer circle and place it on the buttercream to cover the top of the cupcake. Take a palette knife and carefully position a red heart in the centre of the white icing. Press together and smooth over. Decorate all the cupcakes using alternate red and white backgrounds. Keep for 3 days in an airtight container in a cool place.

Bluebird Cupcakes

MAKES 12–14

150 g/5 oz butter, softened
150 g/5 oz caster sugar
150 g/5 oz self-
raising flour
3 medium eggs, beaten

1 tsp lemon juice
1 tbsp milk

To decorate:
125 g/4 oz sugarpaste icing

blue paste food colouring
icing sugar, for dusting
1 batch cream cheese
frosting (*see* page 67)
white gel icing tube

Preheat the oven to 180°C/350°F/Gas Mark 4. Line a 12-hole muffin tray with 12–14 deep paper cases, depending on the depth of the holes.

Place the butter and sugar in a bowl, then sift in the flour. Add the eggs to the bowl with the lemon juice and milk and beat until smooth. Spoon into the cases, filling them three-quarters full.

Bake for about 18 minutes until firm to the touch in the centre. Turn out to cool on a wire rack.

To decorate the cupcakes, colour the sugarpaste blue. Dust a clean flat surface with icing sugar. Roll out the sugarpaste thinly and mark out bird wings in sets of two and one body per bird. Trace round the patterns on page 346 and mark them onto the icing, then stamp out some daisy shapes. Leave all these to dry out for 30 minutes until firm enough to handle.

Swirl the frosting onto each cupcake. Press one bird's body and pair of wings, and some flowers, onto the frosting and pipe on decorations with the white gel icing tubes. Keep in an airtight container in a cool place for 3 days.

For Seasonal Celebrations

Spring Daffodil Cupcakes

MAKES 14

125 g/4 oz self-raising flour
125 g/4 oz caster sugar
125 g/4 oz soft margarine
2 medium eggs, beaten
1 tsp vanilla extract

To decorate:
125 g/4 oz buttercream
 (*see* page 68)
450 g/1 lb ready-to-roll
 sugarpaste

green, yellow and orange
 paste food colouring

Preheat the oven to 180°C/350°F/Gas Mark 4. Line two 12-hole bun trays with 14 paper fairy-cake cases or silicone moulds.

Sift the flour into a bowl and stir together with the caster sugar. Add the margarine, eggs and vanilla extract and beat together for about 2 minutes until smooth.

Spoon into the cases and bake for 15–20 minutes until golden and firm to the touch. Turn out on a wire rack. When cool, trim the tops flat if they have peaked slightly.

To decorate the cupcakes, lightly coat the top of each with a little buttercream. Dust a clean flat surface with icing sugar. Colour half the sugarpaste light green and roll out thinly. Stamp out circles 6 cm/2½ inches wide (*see* page 347) and place these on the buttercream to cover the top of each cupcake.

Colour three quarters of the remaining icing yellow and a quarter orange. Roll out the yellow icing on the paper and mark out thin petal shapes. Take 6 petals and pinch each one together. Place these onto the green icing in a circle, then mould a piece of orange icing into a pea-sized ball. Mould this into a cone shape and place in the centre of the flower. Keep for 3 days in an airtight container.

Easter Nest Cupcakes

MAKES 12

125 g/4 oz soft margarine
125 g/4 oz golden
  caster sugar
150 g/5 oz self-raising flour
2 tbsp cocoa powder
2 medium eggs
1 tbsp golden syrup

To decorate:
1 batch buttercream
  (*see* page 68)
50 g/2 oz shredded
  wheat cereal
125 g/4 oz milk chocolate,
  broken into pieces

25 g/1 oz unsalted butter
chocolate mini eggs

Preheat the oven to 180°C/350°F/Gas Mark 4. Line a 12-hole bun tray with paper cases.

Place the margarine and the sugar in a large bowl, then sift in the flour and cocoa powder. In another bowl, beat the eggs with the syrup, then add to the first bowl. Whisk together with an electric beater for 2 minutes, or by hand with a wooden spoon until smooth.

Divide the mixture between the cases, filling them three-quarters full. Bake for about 15 minutes until they are springy to the touch in the centre. Turn out to cool on a wire rack.

To decorate, swirl the buttercream over the top of each cupcake. Break up the shredded wheat finely. Melt the chocolate with the butter, then stir in the shredded wheat and let cool slightly. Line a plate with clingfilm. Mould the mixture into tiny nest shapes with your fingers, then place them on the lined plate. Freeze for a few minutes to harden. Set a nest on top of each cupcake and fill with mini eggs. Keep for 2 days in a cool place in an airtight container.

Harvest Festival Cupcakes

MAKES 12

175 g/6 oz self-raising
   wholemeal flour
1 tsp baking powder
½ tsp ground cinnamon
pinch salt
150 ml/¼ pint
   sunflower oil

150 g/5 oz soft light
   brown sugar
3 medium eggs, beaten
1 tsp vanilla extract
50 g/2 oz sultanas
225 g/8 oz carrots, peeled
   and finely grated

To decorate:
1 batch cream cheese
   frosting (*see* page 67)
paste food colourings
225 g/8 oz ready-to-roll
   sugarpaste

Preheat the oven to 180°C/350°F/Gas Mark 4. Lightly oil a deep 12-hole muffin tray or line with deep paper cases.

Sift the flour, baking powder and cinnamon into a bowl, along with any bran from the sieve. Add the oil, sugar, eggs, vanilla extract, sultanas and grated carrots.

Beat until smooth and then spoon into the muffin tray. Bake for 20–25 minutes until risen and golden. Cool on a wire rack.

To decorate, colour the frosting pale green and smooth over the top of each cupcake. Colour the sugarpaste in small batches of orange, red, green and brown and mould into cabbages, carrots, potatoes and tomatoes. Press green sugarpaste through a garlic press to make green carrot leaves. Place the vegetables on top of each cupcake. Keep for 3 days in an airtight container in a cool place.

Halloween Cobweb Cupcakes

MAKES 16–18

175 g/6 oz caster sugar
175 g/6 oz soft margarine
3 medium eggs, beaten

150 g/5 oz self-raising flour
1 tsp baking powder
25 g/1 oz cocoa powder

To decorate:
225 g/8 oz icing sugar, sifted
2 tbsp warm water
orange and black paste
    food colourings

Preheat the oven to 180°C/350°F/Gas Mark 4. Line two 12-hole bun trays with 16–18 paper or foil cases, depending on the depth of the holes.

Place the sugar, margarine and eggs in a bowl, then sift in the flour, baking powder and cocoa powder. Beat for 2 minutes or until smooth.

Spoon the mixture into the paper cases and bake for 15–20 minutes until well risen and the tops spring back when lightly pressed. Transfer to a wire rack to cool, then trim the tops of the cupcakes flat if they have any peaks.

To decorate the cupcakes, gradually mix the icing sugar with enough warm water to give a coating consistency. Colour a little of the icing black and place in a small paper icing bag. Colour the remaining icing bright orange.

Work on one cupcake at a time. Spread orange icing over the top of the cupcake. Snip a small hole from the base of the icing bag, then pipe a black spiral on top of the wet orange icing. Use a wooden toothpick and pull this through the icing to give a cobweb effect. Repeat with all the cupcakes and leave to set for 1 hour. Keep for 2 days in an airtight container in a cool place.

Christmas Rose Cupcakes

MAKES 18

150 g/5 oz butter, softened
150 g/5 oz caster sugar
150 g/5 oz self-raising flour
25 g/1 oz ground almonds
3 medium eggs, beaten

1 tsp almond extract
2 tbsp milk

To decorate:
350 g/12 oz sugarpaste

450 g/1 lb fondant icing sugar
125 g/4 oz ready-made
  royal icing
yellow paste food colouring

Preheat the oven to 180°C/350°F/Gas Mark 4. Line two 12-bun trays with 18 silver foil cases.

Place the butter and sugar in a bowl, then sift in the flour and stir in the almonds.
Add the beaten eggs to the bowl with the almond extract and milk and beat until smooth.
Spoon into the cases, filling them three-quarters full.

Bake for about 18 minutes until firm to the touch in the centre. Turn out onto a wire rack.
Once cool, trim the tops of the cupcakes if they have peaked.

To decorate the cupcakes, first line an egg box with kitchen foil and set aside. Roll the
sugarpaste into pea-sized balls and mould each one into a petal shape. Make 4–5 petals
for each cupcake. Place the petals in the egg box to dry out for 2 hours until firm.

Mix the fondant icing sugar with water, according to the packet instructions, to a thick icing of
a spreading consistency. Spread over the top of each cupcake. Work quickly, as the icing will
start to set. Press 4–5 petals into the icing on each cupcake. Colour the royal icing pale
lemon and place in a small paper icing bag and snip off the end. Pipe dots in the centre
of each flower and leave to set for 30 minutes. Keep in a cool place for 2 days.

Sparkly Snowflake Cupcakes

MAKES 24

150 g/5 oz butter, softened
150 g/5 oz caster sugar
150 g/5 oz self-raising flour
25 g/1 oz ground almonds
3 medium eggs, beaten

1 tsp almond extract
1 tbsp milk

To decorate:
icing sugar, for dusting

350 g/12 oz sugarpaste
450 g/1 lb royal icing sugar
edible silver balls

Preheat the oven to 180°C/350°F/Gas Mark 4. Line two 12-bun trays with silver foil cases.

Place the butter and sugar in a bowl, then sift in the flour and stir in the almonds. Add the beaten eggs to the bowl with the almond extract and milk. Spoon into the cases, filling them three-quarters full.

Bake for about 18 minutes until firm to the touch in the centre. Turn out onto a wire rack. Once cool, trim the tops of the cupcakes if they have peaked.

To decorate the cupcakes, dust a clean flat surface with icing sugar. Roll the sugarpaste thinly and trace round the snowflake pattern on page 346. Cut round the shapes and leave them to dry flat on a sheet of nonstick baking parchment for 2 hours until firm.

Make up the royal icing according to the packet instructions to a soft icing that will form peaks. Swirl the icing onto the cupcakes and place a snowflake shape centrally on each cupcake. Decorate with silver balls and leave for 30 minutes to set. Keep for 2 days in an airtight container.

Festive Candy Cane Cupcakes

MAKES 14–18

150 g/5 oz butter, softened
150 g/5 oz caster sugar
150 g/5 oz self-raising flour
25 g/1 oz ground almonds
3 medium eggs, beaten

1 tsp vanilla extract
2 tbsp milk

To decorate:
225 g/8 oz sugarpaste

red and green paste
food colourings
450 g/1 lb royal icing sugar

Preheat the oven to 180°C/350°F/Gas Mark 4. Line two 12-bun trays with 14–18 foil cases, depending on the depth of the holes.

Place the butter and sugar in a bowl, then sift in the flour and stir in the almonds. Add the eggs to the bowl along with the vanilla extract and milk. Spoon into the cases, filling them three-quarters full.

Bake for about 18 minutes until firm to the touch in the centre. Turn out onto a wire rack. Once cool, trim the tops of the cupcakes if they have peaked.

To decorate, colour one quarter of the sugarpaste red and one quarter green. Dust a clean flat surface with icing sugar. Roll out the sugarpaste into long, very thin sausages with the palms of your hands. Roll a sausage of red with a sausage of white to form a twist. Cut into short lengths about 5 cm/2½ inches long and bend round to form a cane shape. Leave to dry out flat for 2 hours until firm.

Make up the royal icing according to the packet instructions to a soft icing that will form peaks. Smooth the icing onto the cupcakes and place a cane centrally on each cupcake. Place the remaining icing in a small piping bag fitted with a star nozzle and pipe a star border round the outside of each cupcake. Keep for 2 days in an airtight container.

Sparkly Christmas Cupcakes

MAKES 14–18

125 g/4 oz butter, softened
125 g/4 oz soft dark
   muscovado sugar
2 medium eggs, beaten
225 g/8 oz self-raising flour
1 tsp ground mixed spice
finely grated zest and 1 tbsp

juice from 1 orange
1 tbsp black treacle
350 g/12 oz mixed dried fruit

To decorate:
3 tbsp sieved apricot glaze
   (*see* page 72)

225 g/8 oz almond paste
   (*see* page 73)
1 batch royal icing
   (*see* page 70)
edible silver ball decorations

Preheat the oven to 180°C/350°F/Gas Mark 4. Line a 12-hole bun tray with 14–18 foil fairy cake cases, depending on the size of the holes.

Beat the butter and sugar together until light and fluffy, then beat in the eggs a little at a time, adding 1 tsp flour with each addition. Sift in the remaining flour and spice, add the orange zest and juice, treacle and dried fruit to the bowl and fold together until the mixture is blended.

Spoon into the cases and bake for about 30 minutes until firm in the centre and a skewer comes out clean. Leave to cool in the tins for 15 minutes, then turn out to cool on a wire rack. Store undecorated in an airtight container for up to 3 weeks, or freeze until needed.

To decorate, trim the top of each fairy cake level if they have peaked, then brush with apricot glaze. Roll out the almond paste and, using the circle on page 347 as a guide, cut out eight circles. Place a disc on top of each fairy cake and press level. Leave to dry for 24 hours if possible.

Swirl the royal icing over the fairy cakes, flicking into peaks with a small palette knife. Decorate with silver balls while the icing is still wet. Leave to dry out for 1 hour. Keep for 4 days in an airtight container.

Gingerbread Cupcakes

MAKES 14–16

8 tbsp golden syrup
125 g/4 oz block margarine
225 g/8 oz plain flour
2 tsp ground ginger

75 g/3 oz sultanas
50 g/2 oz soft dark
   brown sugar
175 ml/6 fl oz milk

1 tsp bicarbonate of soda
1 medium egg, beaten
125 g/4 oz golden icing sugar,
   to decorate

Preheat the oven to 180°C/350°F/Gas Mark 4. Line one or two muffin trays with 14–16 deep paper cases, depending on the size of the holes.

Place the syrup and margarine in a heavy-based pan and melt together gently. Sift the flour and ginger into a bowl, then stir in the sultanas and sugar.

Warm the milk and stir in the bicarbonate of soda. Pour the syrup mixture, the milk and beaten egg into the dry ingredients and beat until smooth.

Spoon the mixture halfway up each case and bake for 25–30 minutes until risen and firm. Cool in the tins for 10 minutes, then turn out to cool on a wire rack.

To decorate the cupcakes, blend the icing sugar with 1 tbsp warm water to make a thin glacé icing. Place in a paper icing bag and snip away the tip. Drizzle over the top of each cupcake in a lacy pattern. Keep in an airtight container for up to 5 days.

Honey Spice Cupcakes

MAKES 12–14

1 tsp instant coffee granules
6 tbsp hot water
175 g/6 oz plain flour
1 tsp baking powder
½ tsp bicarbonate of soda
½ tsp ground cinnamon

½ tsp ground ginger
pinch ground cloves
2 medium eggs
125 g/4 oz golden
    caster sugar
175 g/6 oz honey

5 tbsp vegetable oil
50 g/2 oz walnuts,
    finely chopped
125 g/4 oz golden icing
    sugar, to decorate

Preheat the oven to 160°C/325°F/Gas Mark 3. Line one or two muffin trays with 12–14 deep paper cases, depending on the depth of the holes. Dissolve the coffee in the water and leave aside to cool.

Sift the flour with the baking powder, bicarbonate of soda and spices. In another bowl, beat the eggs with the sugar and honey until smooth and light, then gradually beat in the oil until blended. Stir this into the flour mixture along with the coffee and walnuts. Beat until smooth.

Carefully spoon the mixture into the paper cases. Fill each halfway up. Be careful not to overfill them, as the mixture will rise up. Bake for 25–30 minutes until they are risen, firm and golden. Leave in the tins for 5 minutes, then turn out onto a wire rack to cool.

To decorate, blend the icing sugar with 1 tbsp warm water to make a thin glacé icing. Place in a paper icing bag and snip away the tip. Pipe large daisies round the sides of each cupcake and leave to set for 30 minutes. Keep in an airtight container for up to 5 days.

Scandinavian Apple Cupcakes

MAKES 12–14

125 g/4 oz self-raising flour
½ tsp ground cinnamon
125 g/4 oz caster sugar
125 g/4 oz soft margarine
2 medium eggs, beaten
1 tsp vanilla extract

To decorate:
125 g/4 oz buttercream
  (*see* page 68)

600 g/1 lb 5 oz ready-to-roll
  sugarpaste
red, green and brown paste
  food colourings

Preheat the oven to 180°C/350°F/Gas Mark 4. Line two 12-hole bun trays with red paper or foil cases.

Sift the flour and cinnamon into a bowl and stir together with the caster sugar. Add the margarine and eggs and beat together with the vanilla extract for about 2 minutes until smooth.

Spoon into the cases and bake for 15–20 minutes until golden and firm to the touch. Turn out to cool on a wire rack. When cool, trim the tops flat if they have peaked slightly.

To decorate, lightly coat the top of each cupcake with a little buttercream. Dust a clean flat surface with icing sugar. Colour one quarter of the sugarpaste red, one quarter green and a few scraps brown, leaving the rest white. Roll out the white sugarpaste and stamp out circles 6 cm/2½ inches wide (*see* page 347). Place on top of each cupcake and smooth level. Mould the green and red sugarpaste into round apple shapes and place on top of the white icing. Decorate with small green leaves and brown stalks. Keep for 3 days in an airtight container in a cool place.

Chocolate Holly Leaf Muffins

MAKES 12

125 g/4 oz caster sugar
125 g/4 oz soft tub margarine
2 medium eggs
125 g/4 oz self-raising flour
½ tsp baking powder
50 g/2 oz plain or milk
  chocolate chips

To decorate:
12 holly leaves, washed
  and dried
75 g/3 oz dark
  chocolate, melted
50 g/2 oz unsalted
  butter, softened

300 g/11 oz icing sugar, sifted
125 g/4 oz full-fat
  cream cheese
50 g/2 oz milk chocolate,
  melted and cooled
1 tsp vanilla extract

Preheat the oven to 190°C/375°F/Gas Mark 5. Line a 12-hole muffin tray with deep paper cases.

Place all the cupcake ingredients except the chocolate chips in a large bowl and beat with an electric mixer for about 2 minutes until smooth. Fold in the chocolate chips, then fill the paper cases halfway up with the mixture. Bake for about 15 minutes until firm, risen and golden. Remove to a wire rack to cool.

To decorate the cupcakes, paint the underside of each holly leaf with the melted dark chocolate. Leave to dry out on nonstick baking parchment for 1 hour, or in the refrigerator for 30 minutes.

Beat the butter until soft, then gradually beat in the icing sugar until light. Add the cream cheese and whisk until fluffy. Divide the mixture in half and beat the cooled melted milk chocolate into one half and the vanilla extract into the other half. Fit a piping bag with a wide star nozzle and spoon chocolate icing on one side of the bag and the vanilla icing on the other. Pipe swirls on top of the cupcakes.

Peel the holly leaves away from the set chocolate and decorate the top of each cupcake with a chocolate leaf. Keep for 3 days in an airtight container in a cool place.

Hogmanay Party Cupcakes

MAKES 14

125 g/4 oz self-raising flour
125 g/4 oz caster sugar
125 g/4 oz soft margarine
2 medium eggs, beaten
1 tsp vanilla extract

To decorate:
125 g/4 oz buttercream
  (*see* page 68)
450 g/1 lb ready-to-roll
  sugarpaste

yellow, green and lilac paste
  food colourings

Preheat the oven to 180°C/350°F/Gas Mark 4. Line two 12-hole bun trays with 14 paper fairy-cake cases or silicone moulds.

Sift the flour into a bowl and stir together with the caster sugar. Add the margarine and eggs. Beat with the vanilla extract for about 2 minutes until smooth.

Spoon into the cases and bake for 15–20 minutes until golden and firm to the touch. Turn out onto a wire rack. When cool, trim the tops flat if they have peaked slightly.

To decorate, lightly coat the top of each fairy cake with a little buttercream. Dust a clean flat surface with icing sugar. Colour half the sugarpaste a pale cream shade and roll out thinly. Stamp out circles 6 cm/2½ inches wide (*see* page 347) and place these on the buttercream to cover the top of each fairy cake.

Colour the remaining icing green and lilac. Mould the green icing into stems as pictured or, to be more thistle-like, place a small ball onto each thin stem to form the bulbous part. Mark the bulbous parts of the stems with 'spikes', and position on the fairy cakes. Roll out the lilac sugarpaste into a long thin strip about 2.5 cm/1 inch wide. Cut with a knife, or snip with scissors, three-quarters of the way through the paste, then roll up to form a tassel for a thistle top and attach to the top of a stem. Repeat on all the cakes. Keep for 3 days in an airtight container.

Christmas Tree Cupcakes

MAKES 14

125 g/4 oz self-raising flour
125 g/4 oz caster sugar
125 g/4 oz soft margarine
2 medium eggs, beaten
1 tsp vanilla extract

To decorate:
125 g/4 oz buttercream
(*see* page 68)
600 g/1 lb 5 oz ready-to-roll
sugarpaste

green paste food colouring
edible silver balls

Preheat the oven to 180°C/350°F/Gas Mark 4. Line two 12-hole bun trays with 14 paper fairy-cake cases or silicone moulds.

Sift the flour into a bowl and stir together with the caster sugar. Add the margarine, eggs and vanilla extract and beat together for about 2 minutes until smooth.

Spoon into the cases and bake for 15–20 minutes until golden and firm to the touch. Turn out onto a wire rack. When cool, trim the tops flat if they have peaked slightly.

To decorate, lightly coat the top of each fairy cake with a little buttercream. Colour one quarter of the sugarpaste green and keep aside. Dust a clean flat surface with icing sugar. Roll the white sugarpaste thinly and stamp out 14 circles 6 cm/2½ inches wide (*see* page 347). Set these on the buttercream to cover the top of each fairy cake.

Roll out the green sugarpaste thinly and cut into narrow strips 2.5 cm/1 inch wide. Take a toothpick and roll this back and forth to flute up the edges of the sugarpaste. Cut the fluted strips into graduated layers to make a triangular tree shape and press onto the fairy cake. Decorate with edible silver balls. Keep for 3 days in an airtight container.

Christmas Pudding Cupcakes

MAKES 14–18

125 g/4 oz butter
125 g/4 oz soft dark
  muscovado sugar
2 medium eggs, beaten
225 g/8 oz self-raising flour
1 tsp ground mixed spice
finely grated zest and

1 tbsp juice from 1 orange
1 tbsp black treacle
350 g/12 oz mixed dried fruit

To decorate:
3 tbsp sieved apricot glaze
  (*see* page 72)

225 g/8 oz almond paste
  (*see* page 73)
450 g/1 lb ready-to-roll
  sugarpaste
brown, red, green and yellow
  paste food colourings

Preheat the oven to 180°C/350°F/Gas Mark 4. Line one or two 12-hole bun trays with 14–18 foil fairy-cake cases, depending on the depth of the holes.

Beat the butter and sugar together until light and fluffy, then beat in the eggs a little at a time, adding 1 tsp flour with each addition. Sift in the remaining flour and spice, add the orange zest and juice, treacle and dried fruit to the bowl and fold together until the mixture is blended.

Spoon into the cases and bake for about 30 minutes until firm in the centre and a skewer comes out clean. Leave to cool in the tins for 15 minutes, then turn out to cool on a wire rack. Store undecorated in an airtight container for up to 4 weeks, or freeze until needed.

To decorate, trim the top of each cake level if they have peaked, then brush with apricot glaze. Roll out the almond paste and cut out circles 6 cm/2½ inches wide (*see* page 347). Place a disc on top of each fairy cake and press level. Leave to dry for 24 hours if possible.

Dust a clean flat surface with icing sugar. Colour half the sugarpaste brown, roll out thinly and cut out circles 6 cm/2½ inches wide. Place on top of the almond paste and press level. Colour the remaining sugarpaste cream or pale yellow, mould into a fluted disc and press on top to represent custard. Colour scraps of sugarpaste green and red and shape into holly leaves and berries. Keep for 1 week in an airtight container.

Giftwrapped Presents Cupcakes

MAKES 12–14

125 g/4 oz butter
125 g/4 oz soft dark
     muscovado sugar
2 medium eggs, beaten
225 g/8 oz self-raising flour
1 tsp ground mixed spice
finely grated zest and 1 tbsp

juice from 1 orange
1 tbsp black treacle
350 g/12 oz mixed dried fruit

To decorate:
3 tbsp sieved apricot glaze
  (*see* page 72)

icing sugar, for dusting
600 g/1 lb 5 oz ready-to-roll
     sugarpaste
red, blue, green and yellow
     paste food colourings

Preheat the oven to 180°C/350°F/Gas Mark 4. Line 1 or 2 12-hole muffin trays with 12–14 deep paper cases, depending on the depth of the holes.

Beat the butter and sugar together until light and fluffy, then beat in the eggs a little at a time, adding 1 tsp flour with each addition. Sift in the remaining flour and spice, add the orange zest and juice, treacle and dried fruit to the bowl and fold together until the mixture is blended.

Spoon into the cases and bake for about 30 minutes until firm in the centre and a skewer comes out clean. Leave to cool in the tins for 15 minutes, then turn out to cool on a wire rack. Store undecorated in an airtight container for up to 4 weeks, or freeze until needed.

To decorate, trim the top of each cupcake level if they have peaked, then brush with apricot glaze. Dust a clean flat surface with icing sugar. Colour the sugarpaste in batches and roll out thinly. Cut out circles 6 cm/2½ inches wide (*see* page 347). Place a disc on top of each cupcake and press level. Mould coloured scraps into long thin sausages and roll these out thinly. Place a contrasting colour across each cupcake and arrange into bows and loops. Leave to dry for 24 hours if possible. Keep for 4 days in an airtight container.

Crystallised Rosemary & Cranberry Cupcakes

MAKES 12

125 g/4 oz self-raising flour
125 g/4 oz butter, softened
125 g/4 oz golden caster sugar
2 medium eggs, beaten
zest of ½ orange,
    finely grated

To decorate:
1 egg white
12 small rosemary sprigs
125 g/4 oz fresh red
    cranberries
caster sugar, for dusting

3 tbsp apricot glaze, sieved
    (*see* page 72)
350 g/12 oz ready-to-roll
    sugarpaste

Preheat the oven to 180°C/350°F/Gas Mark 4. Line a 12-hole bun tray with foil fairy cake cases.

Sift the flour into a bowl and add the butter, sugar, eggs and orange zest. Beat for about 2 minutes until smooth, then spoon into the paper cases.

Bake in the centre of the oven for about 14 minutes until well risen and springy in the centre. Transfer to a wire rack to cool.

To decorate, place a sheet of nonstick baking parchment on a flat surface. Beat the egg white until frothy, then brush thinly over the rosemary and cranberries and place them on the nonstick baking parchment. Dust with caster sugar and leave to dry out for 2–4 hours until crisp.

Brush the top of each fairy cake with a little apricot glaze. Roll out the sugarpaste on a clean flat surface dusted with icing sugar and cut out 12 circles 6 cm/2½ inches wide (*see* page 347). Place a disc on top of each and press level. Decorate each one with sparkly rosemary sprigs and cranberries. Keep for 3 days in an airtight container in a cool place.

Glittery Outer Space Cupcakes

MAKES 18–20

125 g/4 oz soft margarine
125 g/4 oz caster sugar
125 g/4 oz self-raising flour
2 medium eggs
1 tsp vanilla extract
1 tbsp milk

To decorate:
125 g/4 oz ready-to-roll
    sugarpaste
edible coloured or glitter dust
1 batch cream cheese
    frosting (*see* page 67)

edible metallic
    coloured balls

Preheat the oven to 180°C/350°F/Gas Mark 4. Line a mini-muffin tray with 18–20 mini paper cases or silicone moulds, depending on the depth of the holes.

Place the margarine and sugar in a bowl, then sift in the flour. In another bowl, beat the eggs with the vanilla extract and milk, then add to the flour mixture. Beat until smooth, then spoon into the cases, filling them halfway up.

Bake for about 12–14 minutes until firm to the touch in the centre. Turn out to cool on a wire rack.

Place a large piece of nonstick baking parchment on a flat surface. Roll the sugarpaste into pea-sized balls on the paper. Coat the balls with edible coloured or glitter dust. Leave to dry out for 2 hours until firm. Place the frosting in a piping bag fitted with a star nozzle and pipe swirls on top of each cupcake. Top each cupcake with the coloured sugarpaste balls and edible metallic balls. Keep for 2 days in an airtight container in a cool place.

White Chocolate Christmas Cupcakes

150 g/5 oz butter, softened
150 g/5 oz caster sugar
150 g/5 oz self-raising flour
3 medium eggs, beaten
1 tsp vanilla extract
1 tbsp milk

75 g/3 oz white chocolate,
 finely grated

To decorate:
250 g/9 oz white
 chocolate, chopped

16 holly leaves, cleaned
 and dried
1 batch buttercream
 (*see* page 68)
icing sugar, for dusting

Preheat the oven to 180°C/350°F/Gas Mark 4. Line one or two 12-hole bun trays with 12–16 foil cases, depending on the depth of the holes.

Place the butter and sugar in a bowl, then sift in the flour. Add the eggs to the bowl with the vanilla extract and milk and beat until smooth. Fold in the grated white chocolate, then spoon into the cases, filling them three-quarters full.

Bake for about 18 minutes until firm to the touch in the centre. Turn out to cool on a wire rack.

To decorate, melt the white chocolate in a heatproof bowl standing over a pan of barely simmering water. Use one third of the melted chocolate to paint the underside of the holly leaves and leave to set for 30 minutes in the refrigerator. Spread one third of the chocolate out onto a clean plastic board. When almost set, make into curls by pulling a sharp knife through the chocolate at an angle until the chocolate curls away from the knife. Stir the remaining cooled chocolate into the buttercream and chill for 15 minutes.

Swirl each cupcake with buttercream, then press on the white chocolate curls. Peel the holly leaves away from the chocolate and carefully place on top of the cupcakes. Dust with icing sugar before serving. Keep for 2 days in the refrigerator.

Savoury Muffins

Pizza Mini Muffins

MAKES 24

15 g/½ oz butter
1 medium onion,
  finely chopped
15 g/½ oz soft sun-dried
  tomatoes, chopped

50 g/2 oz salami, skinned
  and chopped
75 g/3 oz mozzarella
  cheese, grated
1 tbsp fresh basil, chopped

150 g/5 oz plain flour
1½ tsp baking powder
½ tsp salt
1 large egg
125 ml/4 fl oz milk

Preheat the oven to 200°C/400°F/Gas Mark 6. Oil a mini-muffin tray lightly or line with mini paper cases.

Melt the butter in a small pan over a low heat and add the onion. Fry until the onion has softened. Remove to a large bowl and set aside to cool.

Add the chopped tomatoes, salami, half the grated cheese and the basil to the bowl with the onions.

Sift the flour, baking powder and salt into the bowl. In another bowl, beat the egg with the milk and pour into the bowl. Whisk everything with a fork until just combined but still slightly lumpy.

Spoon into the cases and sprinkle each with the remaining mozzarella cheese. Bake for 15–20 minutes until risen and golden. Eat warm or cold on the day of baking.

Peanut Butter Muffins

MAKES 12

125 g/4 oz crunchy
  peanut butter
125 g/4 oz light
  muscovado sugar

50 g/2 oz soft margarine
2 medium eggs
85 ml/3 fl oz milk
150 g/5 oz plain flour

½ tsp baking powder
3 tbsp salted peanuts,
  coarsely chopped

Preheat the oven to 200°C/400°F/Gas Mark 6. Line a deep 12-hole muffin tray with deep paper cases.

In a large bowl, beat the peanut butter, sugar and margarine together until fluffy. In another bowl, whisk the eggs and milk together and set aside. Sift the flour and baking powder into the bowl and then pour in the egg mixture and beat together until smooth.

Spoon into the muffin cases and sprinkle the chopped peanuts over the top of each one.

Bake for about 20 minutes or until well risen and firm to the touch. Turn out to cool on a wire rack and eat warm or cold. Keep for 2 days in an airtight container.

Bacon & Potato Muffins

MAKES 12

225 g/8 oz old-season (baking) potatoes, peeled and cooked
1 medium egg
175 ml/6 fl oz milk

50 ml/2 fl oz sour cream or plain yogurt
3 spring onions, finely sliced
50 g/2 oz Edam cheese, finely grated

75 g/3 oz smoked streaky bacon, trimmed and chopped
175 g/6 oz self-raising flour

Preheat the oven to 200°C/400°F/Gas Mark 6 and line a deep 12-hole muffin tray with deep muffin cases.

Place the cooked potatoes in a large bowl and mash together. Add the egg, milk and sour cream. Stir in the spring onions and half the cheese and bacon. Sift in the flour and stir together until just combined.

Spoon into the muffin cases. Sprinkle over the remaining bacon and grated cheese.

Bake for about 20 minutes until golden, well risen and firm to the touch. Serve warm or cold and eat fresh on the day of baking.

Herb, Onion
& Cheese Mini Muffins

MAKES 12

15 g/½ oz butter
1 medium onion,
    finely chopped
150 g/5 oz plain flour
1½ tsp baking powder

½ tsp salt
1 large egg
125 ml/4 fl oz milk
50 g/2 oz goats' cheese,
    crumbled

1 tbsp each fresh chopped
    parsley and marjoram
50 g/2 oz Edam cheese,
    finely grated

Preheat the oven to 200°C/400°F/Gas Mark 6. Lightly oil a 12-hole mini-muffin tray or line with mini paper cases.

Melt the butter in a small pan over a low heat and fry the onions until softened. Set aside to cool.

Sift the flour, baking powder and salt into a bowl, then beat the egg with the milk in a jug and pour into the flour mixture. Add the goats' cheese, herbs and cooled onions. Mix with a fork until just combined but still slightly lumpy.

Spoon into the cases and sprinkle each muffin with grated Edam cheese. Bake for about 15–20 minutes until risen and golden. Eat warm or cold on the day of baking.

Cheese & Courgette Muffins

MAKES 6

1 medium egg
5 tbsp sunflower oil
6 tbsp milk
½ tsp French mustard
225 g/8 oz plain flour

pinch each salt and
  cayenne pepper
2 tsp baking powder
3 spring onions, chopped
150 g/5 oz courgette,

trimmed and
  coarsely grated
1 tbsp fresh basil, chopped
75 g/3 oz mature Cheddar
  cheese, grated

Preheat the oven to 220°C/425°F/Gas Mark 7. Line a deep 6-hole muffin tray with large paper muffin cases.

Put the egg, oil, milk and mustard in a bowl and whisk with a fork until just blended. Sift in the flour, salt, cayenne pepper and baking powder.

Add the spring onions and courgettes to the bowl with the chopped basil and three quarters of the cheese. Beat the batter together quickly with a fork, being careful not to overmix.

Spoon the mixture into the muffin cases and sprinkle over the remaining cheese. Bake for 15–20 minutes. Serve warm or cold with soup or salad. Eat fresh on the day of baking.

Pesto Muffins

MAKES 20–24

50 g/2 oz butter
225 g/8 oz self-raising flour
1 tsp baking powder
pinch salt

75 g/3 oz mozzarella
  cheese, grated
2 medium eggs
6–7 tbsp milk

1 tbsp green pesto
2 tbsp green olives, chopped
3 tbsp sun-dried
  tomato sauce

Preheat the oven to 180°C/350°F/Gas Mark 4. Lightly oil a mini-muffin tray or line with 20–24 mini cases, depending on the depth of the holes.

Melt the butter over a low heat and leave aside to cool. Sift the flour, baking powder and salt into a bowl and stir in half the mozzarella cheese. In another bowl, beat the eggs with the milk and pesto.

Pour the egg mixture into the flour, then fold in with the cooled butter and chopped olives. Spoon into the muffin cases, then top each one with ½ tsp sun-dried tomato sauce and the remaining grated cheese.

Bake for 15–25 minutes until well risen and golden. Turn out onto a wire rack to cool slightly. Serve warm with soup or salad. Best eaten fresh on the day of baking.

Smoked Ham & Leek Muffins

MAKES 6

50 g/2 oz butter
1 tbsp sunflower oil
1 leek, washed, trimmed and
    thinly sliced
150 g/5 oz plain flour

1 tsp baking powder
½ tsp bicarbonate of soda
1 medium egg, beaten
150ml/½ pint thick
    natural yogurt

75 g/3 oz smoked ham or
    pancetta, finely chopped
few drops Tabasco sauce

Preheat the oven to 200°C/400°F/Gas Mark 6. Oil a deep 6-hole muffin tray or line with deep muffin cases.

Melt the butter over a low heat and set aside to cool. Heat the oil in a small nonstick pan and add the sliced leek. Fry gently for a few minutes to soften, then set aside to cool.

Sift the flour, baking powder and bicarbonate of soda into a bowl. In another bowl, whisk the egg and yogurt together and then pour into the dry ingredients along with the cooled melted butter. Whisk together until just combined, then stir in the leeks and ham and a dash of Tabasco sauce.

Spoon the mixture into the muffin cases and bake for 15–20 minutes until risen and golden brown. Turn out onto a wire rack to cool. Serve warm or cold with soup or salad. Best eaten fresh on the day of baking.

Blue Cheese, Ham & Celery Mini Muffins

MAKES 24

225 g/8 oz self-raising flour
1 tsp baking powder
½ tsp dry mustard powder
pinch salt
50 g/2 oz ham, chopped

75 g/3 oz blue cheese,
    crumbled
2 medium eggs
6 tbsp milk

50 g/2 oz butter, melted
    and cooled
2 celery stalks,
    finely chopped

Preheat the oven to 180°C/350°F/Gas Mark 4. Oil a 24-hole mini-muffin tray or line with 24 mini paper cases.

Sift the flour, baking powder, mustard and salt into a bowl and stir in the ham and half the blue cheese. In another bowl, beat the eggs with the milk and pour into the flour mixture along with the melted butter, then fold in the chopped celery.

Spoon into the muffin cases and then top each one with the remaining blue cheese.

Bake for 15–20 minutes until well risen and golden. Turn out onto a wire rack to cool slightly. Serve warm with cold meats and salad. Best eaten fresh on the day of baking.

Spicy Mini Muffins

MAKES 20–24

1 red pepper
275 g/10 oz plain flour
½ tsp ground smoked paprika
1 tbsp baking powder

2 medium eggs
275 ml/9 fl oz buttermilk
  or yogurt
75 g/3 oz butter,

  melted and cooled
75 g/3 oz chorizo sausage,
  skinned and chopped
dash Tabasco or chilli sauce

Preheat the oven to 200°C/400°F/Gas Mark 6. Lightly oil a 24-hole mini-muffin tray or line with 20–24 mini paper cases, depending on the depth of the holes.

Remove the core and seeds from the pepper and chop the flesh finely. Sift the flour, paprika and baking powder into a bowl and make a well in the centre.

In another bowl, beat the eggs and buttermilk together and pour into the flour mixture along with the melted butter, chorizo and red pepper. Add the Tabasco or chilli sauce and mix until just combined.

Spoon the mixture between the muffin cases and bake for 15–20 minutes until risen and golden brown. Turn out onto a wire rack to cool, then serve warm or cold with soup or salad. Best eaten fresh on the day of baking.

Coriander & Carrot Muffins

MAKES 6

125 g/4 oz plain flour
125 g/4 oz wholemeal flour
1 tbsp baking powder
1 tsp bicarbonate of soda

½ tsp salt
200 ml/7 fl oz milk
1 medium egg, beaten
5 tbsp olive oil

175 g/6 oz carrots, peeled
  and finely grated
3 tbsp fresh coriander,
  finely chopped

Preheat the oven to 190°C/375°F/Gas Mark 5. Oil a deep 6-hole muffin tray or line with deep paper cases.

Sift the flours into a bowl with the baking powder, bicarbonate of soda and salt and add any bran from the sieve.

In another bowl, whisk the milk with the egg and the olive oil and then add to the flour in the bowl. Add the carrots and chopped coriander and stir until just combined.

Spoon the batter into the muffin cases and bake for 20–25 minutes until risen and firm. Turn out to cool on a wire rack, then serve warm or cold with soup or cold meats. Best eaten fresh on the day of baking.

Onion, Soft Cheese & Fig Muffins

MAKES 12

125 g/4 oz butter, melted
1 medium onion, chopped
275 g/10 oz plain flour
1 tbsp baking powder
2 medium eggs

1 tsp Worcestershire sauce
225 ml/8 fl oz milk
125 g/4 oz soft cheese,
   such as Brie or
   Camembert, cubed

125 g/4 oz dried, ready-to-eat
   figs, roughly chopped
1 tbsp flat-leaf parsley,
   chopped

Preheat the oven to 180°C/350°F/Gas Mark 4. Grease a deep 12-hole muffin tray or line with deep muffin cases.

Use a little of the melted butter to fry the chopped onion until softened. Set aside to cool.

Sift the flour and baking powder into a bowl and make a well in the centre. In another bowl, beat the eggs, Worcestershire sauce and milk together and pour into the flour mixture along with the cooled melted butter.

Stir in the fried onions, cubed cheese, chopped figs and parsley until combined and then spoon into the cases. Bake for about 20 minutes until well risen and golden. Turn out to cool on a wire rack and serve with salad or cold meats. Beat eaten on the day of baking.

Bacon & Sweetcorn Muffins

MAKES 8

125 g/ 4 oz rindless smoked
   streaky bacon
3 tbsp sunflower oil
1 small onion, peeled
   and chopped

150 g/5 oz plain flour
2 tsp baking powder
75 g/3 oz frozen
   sweetcorn, thawed
1 medium egg

150 ml/5 fl oz buttermilk
   or natural yogurt
dash of Tabasco sauce

Preheat the oven to 200°C/400°F/Gas Mark 6. Oil a deep 8-hole muffin tray or line with deep paper cases. Chop the bacon and reserve one quarter for garnishing the muffins.

Heat 1 tbsp of the oil over a medium heat and add the onion and bacon. Fry until the bacon is crisp. Leave aside to cool.

Sift the flour and baking powder into a bowl and stir in the bacon and onion mixture and the sweetcorn. In another bowl, beat the egg with the buttermilk or yogurt and the remaining oil and add to the flour mixture with the Tabasco sauce.

Stir together until just combined, then spoon into the muffin trays. Sprinkle over the remaining bacon and bake for about 20 minutes until risen and golden. Eat fresh on the day of baking.

Sweet Muffins

Pistachio Muffins

MAKES 10

125 g/4 oz self-raising flour
125 g/4 oz butter, softened
125 g/4 oz golden
    caster sugar
2 medium eggs, beaten
1 tbsp maple syrup or
    golden syrup

50 g/2 oz pistachio nuts,
    roughly chopped

To decorate:
225 g/8 oz golden icing sugar
125 g/4 oz unsalted
    butter, softened

2 tsp lemon juice
25 g/1 oz pistachio
    nuts, chopped

Preheat the oven to 200°C/400°F/Gas Mark 6. Line a deep 12-hole muffin tray with 10 deep paper cases.

Sift the flour into a bowl and add the butter, sugar and eggs. Beat for about 2 minutes, then fold in the syrup and chopped nuts.

Spoon the mixture into the paper cases and bake for about 20 minutes until well risen and springy in the centre. Remove to a wire rack to cool.

To decorate the cakes, sift the icing sugar into a bowl, then add the butter, lemon juice and 1 tbsp hot water. Beat until light and fluffy, then swirl onto each cupcake with a small palette knife. Place the chopped pistachio nuts in a small shallow bowl. Dip the top of each muffin into the nuts to make an attractive topping. Keep for 4 days in an airtight container in a cool place.

Peaches & Cream Muffins

MAKES 10

225 g/8 oz can peach slices or halves in syrup
125 g/4 oz self-raising flour
50 g/2 oz wholemeal self-raising flour
½ tsp cinnamon

175 g/6 oz butter, softened
175 g/6 oz golden caster sugar
3 medium eggs, beaten
1 tbsp golden syrup

To decorate:
2 tsp lemon juice
2 tbsp icing sugar
150 ml/¼ pint whipping cream

Preheat the oven to 190°C/375°F/Gas Mark 5. Line a deep 12-hole muffin tray with 10 paper cases. Drain the peaches and chop 125 g/4 oz into small chunks.

Sift the flours and cinnamon into a bowl, adding any bran from the sieve, then add the butter, sugar and eggs. Beat for about 2 minutes, then fold in the golden syrup and chopped peaches.

Spoon the mixture into the paper cases and bake for about 20 minutes until well risen and springy in the centre. Remove to a wire rack to cool.

Place 50 g/2 oz sliced peaches in a blender or food processor with the lemon juice and icing sugar to make a purée (the rest of the can's weight is syrup). Whip the cream until it forms soft peaks and then fold in half the purée. Place a large spoonful of cream on top of each muffin, then swirl in a little extra purée. Refrigerate until needed and eat within 24 hours.

Rhubarb & Custard Muffins

MAKES 12

225 g/8 oz pink rhubarb
25 g/1 oz vanilla
   custard powder
175 g/6 oz plain flour
2 tsp baking powder

125 g/4 oz golden
   caster sugar
100 ml/3½ fl oz milk
2 medium eggs, beaten
½ tsp vanilla extract

125 g/4 oz butter, melted
   and cooled
golden caster sugar,
   for dusting

Preheat the oven to 180°C/350°F/Gas Mark 4. Oil or line a 12-hole deep muffin tray with deep muffin cases. Chop the rhubarb into pieces 1 cm/½ inch long.

Sift the custard powder, flour and baking powder into a bowl and stir in the sugar. In another bowl, beat the milk, eggs and vanilla extract together. Make a well in the centre of the dry ingredients and pour in the milk mixture.

Add the melted butter and beat together with a fork until just combined, then fold in the chopped rhubarb. Spoon the mixture into the cases and bake for 15–20 minutes until golden, risen and firm in the centre.

Leave in the tray to firm up for 5 minutes, then turn out onto a wire rack to cool. Serve warm, dusted with golden caster sugar. Eat on the day of baking.

Ginger & Apricot Mini Muffins

MAKES 18

75 g/3 oz plain flour
75 g/3 oz wholemeal flour
2 tsp baking powder
½ tsp ground cinnamon
50 g/2 oz soft light
   brown sugar

1 medium egg
135 ml/4½ fl oz milk
75 g/3 oz butter, melted
125 g/4 oz canned
   apricots, drained and
   finely chopped

50 g/2 oz glacé ginger,
   chopped
50 g/2 oz chopped almonds
sparkly sugar pieces,
   to decorate

Preheat the oven to 200°C/400°F/Gas Mark 6. Line one or two mini-muffin trays with 18 mini paper cases.

Sift the flours, baking powder and cinnamon into a bowl, adding any bran from the sieve, then stir in the sugar. In another bowl, beat the egg and milk together and then pour into the dry ingredients.

Add the melted butter, apricots, ginger and half the almonds and mix quickly with a fork until just combined.

Spoon the mixture into the cases. Scatter the other half of the almonds and the sugar crystals over the top. Bake for 15–20 minutes until risen and golden. Turn out onto a wire rack to cool and eat fresh on the day of baking.

Date, Orange & Walnut Muffins

MAKES 12

275 g/10 oz plain flour
1 tbsp baking powder
125 g/4 oz golden
 caster sugar

175 g/6 oz stoned
 dates, chopped
50 g/2 oz chopped walnuts
1 medium egg

200 ml/7 fl oz milk
finely grated zest and juice
 of 1 orange
6 tbsp sunflower oil

Preheat the oven to 200°C/400°F/Gas Mark 6. Line a deep 12-hole muffin tray with deep paper cases.

Sift the flour and baking powder into a bowl and make a well in the centre.

Add all the remaining ingredients and beat together until just combined. Spoon the batter into the paper cases and bake for about 16–18 minutes until well risen and firm to the touch.

Serve warm or cold and eat the muffins on the day of baking.

Streusel–Topped Banana Muffins

MAKES 6

To decorate:
25 g/1 oz self-raising flour
15 g/½ oz butter
40 g/1½ oz demerara sugar
½ tsp ground cinnamon

To make the muffins:
125 g/4 oz self-raising
  wholemeal flour
25 g/1 oz plain flour
2 medium ripe bananas,
  about 175 g/6 oz

1 large egg
50 ml/2 fl oz sunflower oil
50 ml/2 fl oz milk

Preheat the oven to 200°C/400°F/Gas Mark 6. Line a deep muffin tray with 6 deep paper cases. Make the topping first by rubbing the butter into the flour until it resembles fine crumbs. Stir in the sugar and cinnamon and set aside.

To make the muffins, sift the flours into a bowl, then make a well in the centre. Mash the bananas with a fork and add them to the bowl.

In another bowl, beat the egg, oil and milk together and then add them to the bowl. Mix together until evenly blended, then spoon into the muffin cases, filling them two-thirds full.

Sprinkle the streusel topping over each muffin and bake for about 25 minutes until golden and a skewer inserted into the centre comes out clean. Eat fresh on the day of baking.

Coconut & Lime Muffins

MAKES 12

125 g/4 oz soft margarine
125 g/4 oz golden
    caster sugar
2 medium eggs
50 g/2 oz desiccated coconut

1 lime
125 g/4 oz self-raising flour
1 tsp baking powder
2 tbsp milk

To decorate:
40 g/1½ oz unsalted butter
125 g/4 oz icing sugar
50 g/2 oz coconut chips
zest of 1 lime, grated

Preheat the oven to 180°C/350°F/Gas Mark 4. Line a deep 12-hole muffin tray with deep paper cases.

Place the margarine and caster sugar in a bowl and add the eggs and coconut. Finely grate the zest from the lime into the bowl, then squeeze in the juice. Sift in the flour and baking powder.

Add the milk and whisk together for about 2 minutes with an electric beater, or by hand until smooth, then spoon into the paper cases. Bake for 15–20 minutes until golden and firm. Cool on a wire rack.

To decorate the muffins, beat the butter and icing sugar together until smooth, then pipe or swirl onto each muffin. Press the coconut chips into the buttercream and then scatter the grated lime zest on top. Keep for 3 days in an airtight container in a cool place.

Tropical Mango Muffins

MAKES 10

50 g/2 oz soft dried
pineapple chunks
50 g/2 oz soft dried
papaya pieces
25 g/1 oz soft dried
mango pieces

225 g/8 oz plain flour
1 tsp baking powder
½ tsp bicarbonate of soda
75 g/3 oz golden
caster sugar
1 medium egg

275 ml/9 fl oz milk
zest and 1 tbsp juice from
1 small orange
50 g/2 oz butter, melted
and cooled

Preheat the oven to 200°C/400°F/Gas Mark 6. Line a deep muffin tray with 10 deep paper muffin cases. Wet a sharp knife and chop the fruits into small chunks. Set them aside.

Sift the flour, baking powder and bicarbonate of soda into a large bowl. Add the sugar and make a well in the centre. In another bowl, beat the egg and milk together with the orange juice.

Add the milk to the bowl with the melted butter and the orange zest and beat with a fork until all the flour is combined but the mixture is still slightly lumpy. Fold in three-quarters of the chopped fruit and spoon into the paper cases. Sprinkle the remaining fruit over the top of each muffin.

Bake for about 20 minutes until risen, golden and firm. Cool on a wire rack and eat warm or cold. Keep for 24 hours sealed in an airtight container.

Simnel Easter Muffins

MAKES 6–8

125 g/4 oz yellow marzipan
150 ml/¼ pint milk
50 g/2 oz soft light
   brown sugar

2 medium eggs
175 g/6 oz self-raising flour
½ tsp mixed spice
75 g/3 oz mixed dried fruit

50 g/2 oz glacé cherries,
   washed and chopped
75 g/3 oz butter, melted
   and cooled

Preheat the oven to 190°C/375°F/Gas Mark 5. Line a deep muffin tray with 6–8 paper cases, depending on the depth of the holes. Weigh 25 g/1 oz of the marzipan and roll into long thin strips. Grate or chop the remaining marzipan into small chunks.

Whisk the milk, sugar and eggs together in a jug. Sift the flour and spice into a bowl, then stir together with the fruit, cherries and the marzipan chunks. Pour the milk mixture into the flour mixture along with the melted butter. Mix until combined.

Spoon into the paper cases and make a cross over the top of each using two marzipan strips. Bake for about 20 minutes until firm in the centre. Cool in the tins for 3 minutes, then turn out to cool on a wire rack. Eat warm or cold. Keep for 24 hours sealed in an airtight container.

Blueberry Buttermilk Muffins

MAKES 6–8

175 g/6 oz plain flour
1 tsp baking powder
175 g/6 oz golden caster sugar

175 ml/6 fl oz buttermilk
1 medium egg
½ tsp vanilla extract

40 g/1½ oz butter, melted
   and cooled
150 g/5 oz fresh blueberries

Preheat the oven to 180°C/350°F/Gas Mark 4. Line a deep muffin tray with 6–8 paper cases, depending on the depth of the holes.

Sift the flour and baking powder into a bowl, then add the sugar. In another bowl, beat the buttermilk with the egg and vanilla extract, then pour into the dry ingredients. Mix with a fork, then add the cooled melted butter and stir until mixed but still slightly lumpy.

Gently fold in the blueberries. Spoon the mixture into the muffin cases, filling each two-thirds full. Bake for about 20 minutes until springy in the centre. Leave in the trays for 5 minutes, then turn out onto a wire rack to finish cooling. Eat warm or cold on the day of baking.

Chocolate Chip Cherry Muffins

MAKES 12

75 g/3 oz glacé cherries
75 g/3 oz milk or dark
   chocolate chips
75 g/3 oz soft margarine

200 g/7 oz caster sugar
2 medium eggs
150 ml/¼ pint thickset
   natural yogurt

5 tbsp milk
275 g/10 oz plain flour
1 tsp bicarbonate of soda

Preheat the oven to 200°C/400°F/Gas Mark 6. Line a deep 12-hole muffin tray with deep paper cases. Wash and dry the cherries. Chop them roughly, mix them with the chocolate chips and set aside.

Beat the margarine and sugar together, then whisk in the eggs, yogurt and milk. Sift in the flour and bicarbonate of soda. Stir until just combined.

Fold in three-quarters of the cherries and chocolate chips. Spoon the mixture into the cases, filling them two-thirds full. Sprinkle the remaining cherries and chocolate chips over the top.

Bake for about 20 minutes until golden and firm. Leave in the tins for 4 minutes, then turn out to cool on a wire rack. Serve straight away or keep for 24 hours in an airtight container.

Very Berry Muffins

MAKES 10

225 g/8 oz plain flour
1 tsp baking powder
½ tsp bicarbonate of soda
65 g/2½ oz golden caster sugar

1 medium egg
175 ml/6 fl oz milk
zest and 1 tbsp juice from
    1 small orange

50 g/2 oz butter, melted
    and cooled
125 g/4 oz fresh raspberries
50 g/ 2 oz dried cranberries

Preheat the oven to 200°C/400°F/Gas Mark 6. Line a deep 12-hole muffin tray with 10 deep paper cases.

Sift the flour, baking powder and bicarbonate of soda into a large bowl. Add the sugar and make a well in the centre. Beat the egg and milk together in a jug with the orange juice.

Pour the milk mixture into the bowl together with the cooled butter and the orange zest and beat lightly with a fork until all the flour is combined but the mixture is still slightly lumpy. Gently fold in the raspberries and cranberries and spoon into the paper cases.

Bake for about 20 minutes until firm and risen and a skewer inserted into the centre comes out clean. Cool on a wire rack. Eat warm or cold on the day of baking.

Coffee & Walnut Muffins

MAKES 12

125 g/4 oz butter, softened
125 g/4 oz soft light
  brown sugar
150 g/5 oz plain flour
1 tsp baking powder
2 medium eggs

1 tbsp golden syrup
1 tsp vanilla extract
4 tbsp sour cream
40 g/1½ oz walnut pieces,
  chopped

To decorate:
150 ml/¼ pint double cream
1 tbsp golden caster sugar
1 tsp coffee extract
½ tsp ground cinnamon
50 g/2 oz walnut pieces

Preheat the oven to 180°C/350°F/Gas Mark 4. Grease or line a 12-hole muffin tray with paper cases.

Beat the butter and sugar together until light and fluffy. Sift in the flour and baking powder, then add the eggs, golden syrup, vanilla extract and soured cream. Beat together until fluffy, then fold in the nuts.

Spoon the batter into the paper cases, filling them about three-quarters full. Bake for about 25 minutes until a skewer inserted into the centre comes out clean. Turn out to cool on a wire rack.

For the topping, put the cream, sugar, coffee extract and cinnamon in a bowl and whisk until soft peaks form. Swirl over the muffins and top each with a walnut piece. Refrigerate until needed, or keep chilled for 24 hours in an airtight container.

Blackcurrant & Lemon Muffins

MAKES 12

1 lemon
275 g/10 oz plain flour
1 tbsp baking powder
125 g/4 oz caster sugar

2 medium eggs
275 ml/9 fl oz milk
½ tsp vanilla extract

75 g/3 oz butter, melted
  and cooled
150 g/5 oz fresh or frozen
  blackcurrants, trimmed

Preheat the oven to 200°C/400°F/Gas Mark 6. Grease or line a deep 12-hole muffin tray with deep paper cases.

Finely grate the zest from the lemon into a bowl, then sift in the flour and baking powder and stir in the sugar. In another bowl, beat the eggs with the milk and vanilla extract.

Make a well in the centre and pour in the egg mixture and the cooled melted butter. Stir together with a fork until just combined and then gently fold in the blackcurrants.

Spoon into the muffin trays and bake for 20 minutes or until firm and golden. Leave in the tins for 4 minutes, then turn out onto a wire rack to finish cooling. Serve warm or cold. Best eaten on the day of baking.

Fruity Buttermilk Muffins

MAKES 12

175 g/6 oz self-raising flour
50 g/2 oz wholemeal self-
    raising flour
1 tsp mixed ground spice
½ tsp bicarbonate of soda
1 medium egg

2 tbsp fine-cut orange
    shred marmalade
125 ml/4 fl oz milk
50 ml/2 fl oz buttermilk
5 tbsp sunflower oil

125 g/4 oz eating apple,
    peeled, cored and diced
125 g/4 oz ready-to-eat pitted
    prunes, roughly chopped

Preheat the oven to 200°C/400°F/Gas Mark 6. Line a deep 12-hole muffin tray with deep paper cases.

Sift the flours, spice and bicarbonate of soda into a bowl. In another bowl, beat the egg with the marmalade, milk, buttermilk and oil and pour into the dry ingredients.

Stir with a fork until just combined, then fold in the apple and chopped prunes. Spoon into the cases and bake for about 20 minutes until golden, risen and firm to the touch.

Leave in the tins for 4 minutes, then turn out onto a wire rack to finish cooling. Serve warm or cold and eat on the day of baking.

Pineapple, Cream Cheese & Carrot Muffins

MAKES 12

175 g/6 oz self-raising wholemeal flour
1 tsp baking powder
½ tsp ground cinnamon
pinch salt
150 ml/¼ pint sunflower oil

150 g/5 oz soft light brown sugar
3 medium eggs, beaten
50 g/2 oz soft dried pineapple, chopped
225 g/8 oz carrots, peeled and finely grated

To decorate:
75 g/3 oz cream cheese
175 g/6 oz golden icing sugar
2 tsp lemon juice
50 g/2 oz soft dried pineapple pieces, thinly sliced

Preheat the oven to 180°C/350°F/Gas Mark 4. Lightly oil a deep 12-hole muffin tray or line with deep paper cases.

Sift the flour, baking powder, cinnamon and salt into a bowl, including any bran from the sieve. Add the oil, sugar, eggs, chopped pineapple and grated carrots.

Beat until smooth, then spoon into the muffin cases. Bake for 20–25 minutes until risen and golden. Cool on a wire rack.

To decorate the muffins, beat the cream cheese and icing sugar together with the lemon juice to make a spreading consistency. Swirl the icing over the top of each cupcake, then top with a piece of dried pineapple. If chilled and sealed in an airtight container, these will keep for 3–4 days.

Templates for Sugarpaste Shapes

On these pages, you will find templates for some of the icing shapes as used in this book. Templates such as these are handy if you do not have a selection of metal cutters. Just trace the pattern you want onto a sheet of clear greaseproof paper or nonstick baking parchment. Roll out the sugarpaste thinly, then position the traced pattern over the icing. Mark over the pattern with the tip of a small sharp knife or a pin. Remove the paper and cut out the marked-on pattern with a small sharp knife. Voilà!

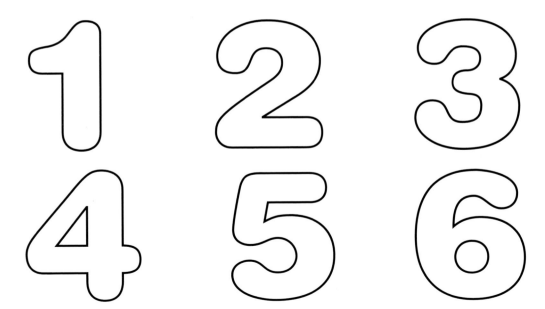

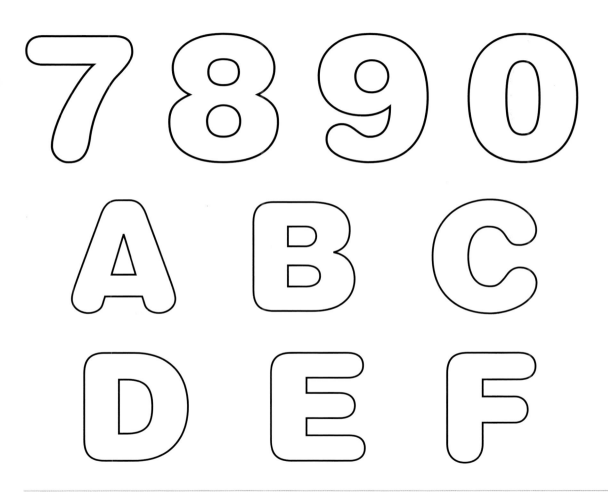

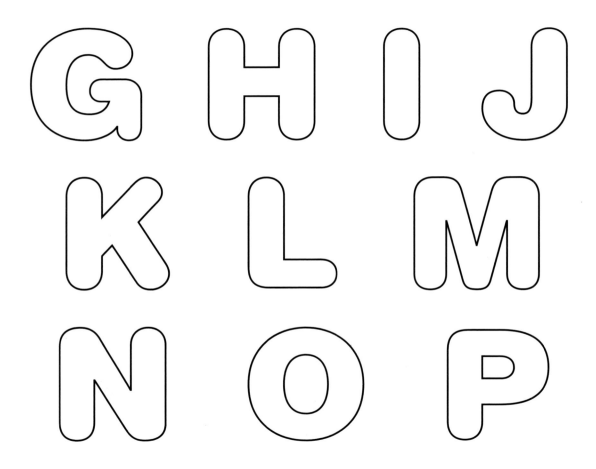

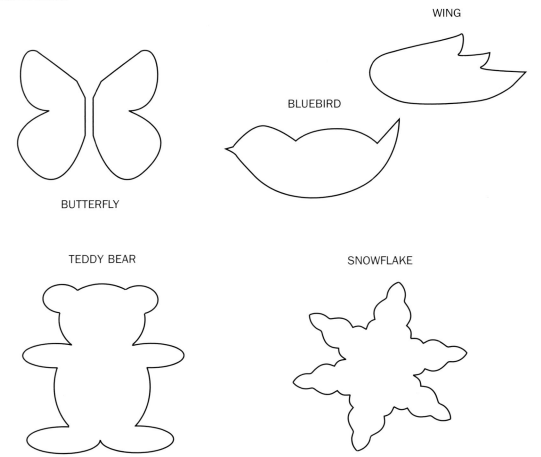

WING

BLUEBIRD

BUTTERFLY

TEDDY BEAR

SNOWFLAKE

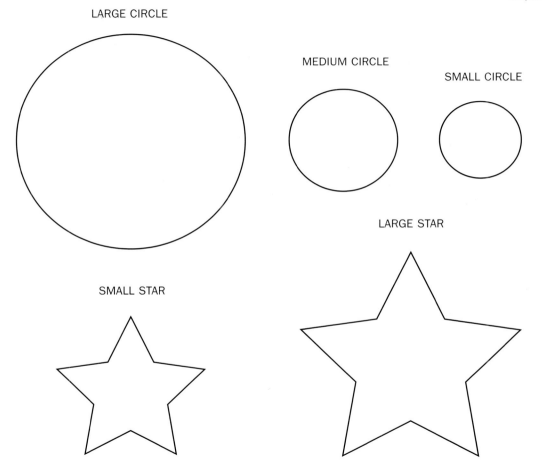

LARGE CIRCLE

MEDIUM CIRCLE

SMALL CIRCLE

LARGE STAR

SMALL STAR

LARGE HEART

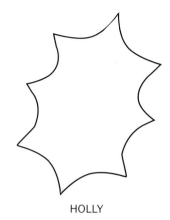

HOLLY

MEDIUM HEART

SMALL HEART

IVY

FLOWER

CAR

PETAL & LARGE BUTTERFLY WING

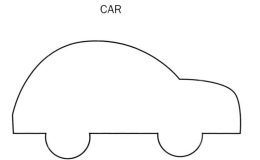

Index